Angel Healing
& Alchemy – How to Begin

Melchisadec, Sacred Seven & the Violet Ray

Angel Healing & Alchemy – How to Begin

Melchisadec, Sacred Seven & the Violet Ray

Angela McGerr

AXIS MUNDI
BOOKS

Winchester, UK
Washington, USA

First published by Axis Mundi Books, 2015
Axis Mundi Books is an imprint of John Hunt Publishing Ltd., Laurel House, Station Approach,
Alresford, Hants, SO24 9JH, UK
office1@jhpbooks.net
www.johnhuntpublishing.com
www.axismundi-books.com

For distributor details and how to order please visit the 'Ordering' section on our website.

Design: Stuart Davies
www.stuartdaviesart.com

Printed and bound by CPI Group (UK) Ltd, Croydon, CR0 4YY, UK

We operate a distinctive and ethical publishing philosophy in all
areas of our business, from our global network of authors to
production and worldwide distribution.

CONTENTS

Sacred Seven – Angel Healing and Alchemy

SEVEN: The sacred number of spiritual alchemy and healing ruled by Melchisadec, Prince of Peace. SEVEN are his Rulers of the Weekdays. SEVEN is the traditional Rainbow (first SEVEN major chakras of healing) and his is the SEVENTH Ray of Violet offering alchemy through Love (pink) and Truth (blue). SEVEN are the turns of his Cretan Labyrinth which is the path by which we re-find True Self. SEVEN is the hidden Violet point in the Macrocosm (All That Is - Six Point Star). This is the point of Melchisadec which some term Source as it brings transcendence over time, space and matter. SEVEN, the number of Magic and Mystery, also signifies the Mystery Schools, embraces all their ancient wisdom, and so offers spiritual awakening, development and fulfilment. In fact SEVEN engenders spiritual alchemy. Therefore, if you choose to work with SEVEN you are fast-tracked by the angels, under the personal direction of Melchisadec himself, along the mystical Way of Love and Light.

General Introduction to Angelology and Alchemy

Welcome to a practice first documented by the Essenes around 2,000 years ago: that of communing daily with angels so that they support us to reach a state of physical and spiritual harmony in life. Angela McGerr Angelology is a simplified 21st Century form of this spiritual discipline, interwoven with angels from other belief systems, and blended with the alchemy found in Hermetic philosophy, which comprises the Love, Power and Wisdom of Hermes Trismegistus.

This is nothing to do with the alchemy of lead to gold! Though many pursued this and termed it The Great Work, it was also used as a cover for the teaching of the ancient mysteries. Always of great spiritual validity, these were regarded as heresy in past centuries, and punishable by death.

It is to some of these ancient mysteries that we return in this book, with a particular focus on Sacred Seven, and the Seventh Ray of Violet which is an alchemy ray in terms of transmuting negative energies in life in order to make spiritual progress. Basically, this book propounds a healing system you can work with every day, using angelic support to enrich and even transform self and life, and it is how I changed my own life beginning back in 1999. Furthermore, there are many levels to attain. However, what you receive from this book (and Melchisadec and his angels) will depend entirely on what you, yourself, put into it. *I ask you to bear this in mind because it is for you to choose whether or not you make a firm commitment to work daily with these angels.* If you do, you will firstly make a personal connection to each of them. Secondly, as you continue working with this book you will gradually deepen your angelic links, because, thirdly, you will begin to raise your own vibration closer to theirs.

How? You will develop your personal "clair" skill (clairsen-tience, clairaudience, clairvoyance). I am not clair*voyant* myself and the good news is that it is certainly not necessary to be clair-voyant to work with angels every day; the other "clairs" are just as effective, open to everyone, and all will be explained.

Optional Angelic Light Attunements

With loving will and intention I have created, and placed sublim-inally, an Angelic Light Attunement for you to receive only if your heart and soul so chooses. This will connect you to Melchisadec and each of his Sacred Seven. These attunements exist in the ether (Spirit) where time is non-linear. By this I mean they exist outside of Space/Time as generally perceived. If you wish to take advantage of this offer, and you commit through Love to working with each angel, the angel will allow you to make this Light connection to advance your own spiritual devel-opment. Guidance is given in each chapter about this.

The high vibration of angels (Angelic Light) is rather like a "long-distance" energy connection to most people. However, by the grace of the angels and their loving support, but even more importantly, if your own heart commits, I have willed and intended the book to contain the means of making the connection "local" for you, so long as it is for your Highest Good. This is the first and simplest of Angelic Light Attunements that are possible, and that I have been giving to students (in person or "distantly") for many years. More complex attunements confer levels of healing skills. For more on how I (or rather the angels through me) set up these attunements in Templa Mar: the etheric healing Temple of the Emerald Sea, please consult the Appendix.

The subliminal attunement offers a continuous connection to each angel in this book, opening a Door to Light for you. Through it you can draw loving angelic support to commence a brand new healing opportunity for self and life. This includes cleansing and unblocking various chakra energy centres that are the remit of the Sacred Seven (*other chakras are addressed by the Rulers of the Elements: Ariel, Uriel, Phuel, and Seraphiel*). The unblocking of these chakras by the Sacred Seven balances karma and helps release ancient vows and ties, therefore raising your spiritual consciousness. I believe it is only since the year 2000 that there has been a critical mass of Love and Light (generated by healers and those just sending out loving compassion from the heart) to raise Mother Earth's own vibration sufficiently to make this possible. Everything is about free will and there have never been more choices for you.

Spiritual alchemy

The support of the angels is always and only about healing at one level or another to engender spiritual progress; this is their remit from God/The Creator. However, by simply working with this book you have already indicated at soul level to Melchisadec and his Sacred Seven Angels that you wish to self-heal towards inner peace and harmony (what I term your Heart Quest) and perhaps even more importantly, to perhaps help guide others in similar healing (your soul purpose or Soul Quest).

Love is the key. Through each of their unique Angelic Light vibrations, coupled with your loving will and intention to reach towards them, the angels will support you to build your personal angelic links. The purpose of these is to aid you to heal physically, mentally and emotionally to a new and higher level of harmony; I call this the Dance of Six, as it links to the Six Point Star (Macrocosm) which is the symbol of wholeness, completion and balance and explained later in the book. Thus healed you can then grow to a new and higher *spiritual* level – spiritual alchemy indeed. That part of the process is linked to the Five Point Star (Microcosm) – the symbol of our spiritual growth. I call this the Dance of Five, also fully explained later, but it is a Dance because the two numbers interchange as you work at this spiritual advancement, first Six and then Five; then Six again and so on. The more you wish to connect and work with these Light Beings on this (both for yourself, and for others – to help them find inner peace) the more you will sense their support.

Understanding Angelic Numerology

As mentioned above with the Dance, this book also guides on Angelic Numerology, as this is hugely important; when you grasp the significance of certain numbers they offer you daily signs for healing and raising vibration towards (and beyond) Ascension.

We begin with The Law of Three, as this is how the angels taught me to manifest their rays so that I could develop my "clair" skills and feel the energy for myself. Then we must bring Four (Love – heart chakra) into the equation as we progress our Dance of Six and Five. However, in this book the focus is on Seven, a number of Mystery and Magic that weaves into our healing and harmony and, when integrated (through the continuing Dance of Six and Five), leads us on to the higher sacred numbers of Eight, Nine, and finally to the higher Dance of Twelve and Thirteen.

In Cassiel's chapter you will find more on Angelic Numerology to guide daily life.

Physical and spiritual harmony

In summary, then, the angels see and know all our actions (this is their role as tasked by the Creator) and they are filled with joy when we focus with their aid on attaining physical and spiritual harmony. However, in this reality, because *we have been given free will*, it is always our decision how we use the opportunities offered. When we *choose to invite angelic Light Beings into our lives every day* then they willingly support our spiritual development with their unconditional Love.

I really hope you will find this Angelology self-help book enjoyable and enriching and want to try all the meditations and exercises. Although it is self-study and you can work with it at your own pace, you are urged to keep building knowledge and energy; this is a gradual process and there are no quick fixes! Yet you are not doing this unaided – remember you are never alone when you have invoked the angels, especially the angel ruling the day on which you are working with the material, as well as your own Primary Guardian (Ruler of the weekday on which you were born.) I will come back to this later.

Finding the Way of Love & Light

Even if you just take the time to read through this book, there are likely to be subtle, subliminal changes in yourself and your life. But what really counts is *living this truth of Angelology,* and what transforms you is *your learning how to make your own daily connection with the angels.* This is the first of many healing steps you can take along The Way of Love & Light, that gradually guide you to that elusive inner peace and harmony.

If you then begin to send out waves of Love & Light from your heart, as it opens, this will benefit mankind, Mother Earth and All Life. Only by doing this do we begin to appreciate just how powerful a loving will and intention can be, if we have a sincere desire to help others.

I would, however, point out that huge as this realisation is, it is only *the very first step on the Way.* If you continue to work with angels, your spiritual Dance of Six and Five will gather pace, and you will have the wondrous opportunity to become a conduit in the re-uniting of the polarities of Above and Below.

Limitless potential

To say it's the beginning is a serious understatement! After Melchisadec and his Sacred Seven, you could learn about his Sacred Nine, using nine of Twelve Colours of Creation in different vibrations and to new healing levels. This brings in the expanded Rainbow of Melchisadec, 3D sacred geometry (Star

Tetrahedron) and the Rulers of the Elements: Ariel, Uriel and Phuel. Higher stages of vibration cover white Gold and white Silver with Shekinah and Metatron respectively (Ten and Eleven), and how White Fire radiates from their Sacred Eden Tree.

You can learn how to access and channel Seraphiel's Diamond Rays of Creation (Twelve) and also his Sacred Thirteen, including the twin, hidden, Zodiac Gateways of Hermes Trismegistus (Ophiucus or Dragon) and Pistis Sophia (Delphinus or Dolphin). There are various ways to regain Oneness with All and to manifest this to help others find the Way. You become (in your etheric – spirit self) very tall indeed: your root chakra stretches down to the heart of Mother Earth, your higher heart chakra interfaces with Templa Mar* and your crown chakra touches the 44:44 Angel Star Gate of heart – master portal to unfallen, pure Angelic Light. Yet even that, believe it or not, is but another step on the Way, and I tell you more in the concluding chapter of this book. The most important thing is to get started on the journey!

*see also my previous nine books and card sets: Angel Quest of the Heart, Heart & Soul Angel Cards, Love & Light Angel Cards, website etc and final chapter, before Appendix.

Chapter One

Angelology for Physical/Spiritual Harmony

About Angels and Angelology

To begin at the beginning, although they can and do sometimes appear in humanoid form, I do not believe that this is what angels really are; they have no need of bodies or genders, for they are pure energy – Angelic Light – at its highest vibration, next to that of the Diamond Ray of God/The Creator, carried by the Seraphim Creation Angels. In other words angels are God's messengers who have been tasked to aid mankind's spiritual growth. In fact they can and do appear in many forms, as necessary, and we gain comfort by thinking of them in terms of genders. If we need them to appear in humanoid form, so that we recognise them as angels, then they do so. However, in general, in my personal experience, they manifest in more subtle ways such as an angelic flower scent, warm, cool or tingling energy, white Light flashing in the mind, small balls of coloured Light, a light touch on face or body, a feeling like being swathed in soft feathers (more on this later). But although the role of the angels is to support us in our life path, with particular reference to guiding our spiritual development, *they are not allowed to directly influence our lives unless we invite them in*, so each of us has a choice to make about this.

We can read about angels in an abstract way, and envy those who can see them around us, or we can approach this positively by learning a different way of communicating with angels, to then be able to directly ask for, and feel their loving support of us. To really work with angels we need to make them our friends, and we definitely need to talk to them daily. Angelology is the term used for communing (invoking and working) with angels every day. I mentioned the Essenes in the introduction about

Angelology. As as a key part of their spiritual practices, the Essenes believed that to attain and maintain physical and spiritual harmony one called on angels daily for assistance, and as part of that practice, they identified Angel Rulers for each weekday (linked to the Solar System) on whom they could focus. These are termed the Sacred Seven Angels (and seven: the number of Magic and Mystery is sacred in almost all belief systems).

Then, as now, we can tune in to the power of seven and the alchemy that it offers. As tasked by Melchisadec, each of the Sacred Seven brings different life attributes to us, linked to reaching our next stage of healing and wholeness, (Dance of Six) and so over the course of the week, we can tackle, in turn, all our various, major life issues. At the same time, by reaching that stage, we are then able to grow to our next spiritual level (Dance of Five). Not only that, but another purpose of this book is for you to meet and greet *the Angel Ruler of the day of the week on which you were born*: this is your own Primary Guardian.

Although I have, of necessity, simplified Essene Angelology for 21st Century readers, I retained the basic philosophy of working daily with the seven ruling angels, and their recorded focuses, because this is still equally valid two millennia later, *if* we are prepared to work at it. These wonderful beings of Love and Light that we call angels have always been, and will always be around us, waiting for our call, to be invited to come with their individual qualities to support us in life. To work with the angels is to begin to travel their spiritual Way of Love and Light. By adding the angels to our daily existence, we are safely guided on moving through physical and emotional issues and releasing blocks and limiting mindsets (sometimes from past lives) in order to allow new spiritual development. And so we begin to attain that inner peace found through greater physical/spiritual harmony. I did exactly this myself and my life changed totally from that day on. This book tells you how you can start your own transformational journey on the Way, as I did myself back in 1999, and have continued to do ever since.

Ancient Wisdom – A brief history of Winged Messengers

How old is the concept of Winged Messengers? Most of our angel wisdom on guardianships comes from the Dead Sea Scrolls, (particularly the Jubilee Scroll) almost certainly written by the Essenes. However, when I researched this back in 1999 I found that the concept goes back much further – to the dawn of recorded time. Angels (though the name itself changes) are in almost all religions or belief systems, but actually they pre-date most religions by thousands of years. If you are Christian, Moslem or Jewish, you will already know about some angels (although that name – *angelos* – derives from the Greek, meaning messenger). But if you lived in Ancient Egypt, you would be aware of Egyptian angels, such as Ma'at. In Persia, Zoroaster's angels (amesha spentas) date back at least four thousand years, while cylinder seals and stone blocks with carvings of winged beings have been found from Sumeria and are believed to date back around six thousand years.

Actually I think angels existed long before that, and there are winged glyphs/pictograms carved in stone that are believed to be 25,000 – 50,000 years old and Lemurian (or Mu*). It seems that throughout the history of man there have been hundreds of winged Light Beings aiding us, including our various assigned Guardian Angels. If you are not religious in the traditional sense, this is perfectly fine, as the angels bring, and support us with, the prospect of personal spiritual progress, at our own pace, and in our own chosen fashion. *See books by Colonel James Churchward*

Modern Wisdom – How to "know" if angels are around us

There are already many forms of energy in this world that cannot be seen with the eye – yet we readily accept they exist. We know what this energy can do, because we can directly *feel or see the effect of it.* The objective of this book is to teach you not only how to feel/sense the effects of this form of energy that is the Angelic Light vibration so that you can accept angels are present, but also to show you how you can work actively with them and with that vibration to support your own self-healing.

What you first need to realise is everything that exists, including mankind, is comprised only of energy in some form of vibration. In general (and because of the various "Falls from Grace"), mankind's vibration is quite low (or dense). On the other hand, that of the angels is ultra-high and pure; it's second only to that of the Creator: radiating full power of unconditional Love through a pure (unfallen, or Metatronic) Light spectrum. In fact the way I put it is that it is Love giving form to Light.

To connect with/sense/detect angels we just need to raise our game in terms of vibration, or, to look at it another way, we need to raise our spiritual perception and expand our own, personal belief system.

Angels exist around us all the time, but most of us are unaware of them, firstly because of the vast difference in our vibration compared to theirs, and secondly because most of us are *not* born with the psychic or 6th Sense "clair" skills to see/feel/hear them. To "see" angels in every-day life you need the psychic skill of clair-*voyance*, and 99 per cent of us were not born with that gift. People with clairvoyant ability can "see" beyond the visible in this world, in other words beyond the usual human energy vibration. What they "see" depends on their level of skill, and indeed can be frightening to a child because there are lots of different vibrations (rather like layers) beyond our own and because the spirit world is said to be able to detect who can "see".

Moving on from there, the good news is that there are other types of "clair" skills that you can actually train, just as you would any other skill. For what you may also not realise (and I didn't either when this all began) is that while 99 per cent of us are not born clairvoyant, from my own personal experience I have found we all have, or can acquire, other psychic skills. It probably starts with what we call our intuition, which is a heart-based attribute. On learning a methodology, with practice, over 99 per cent of us can become clair-*sentient* and feel/sense angel energy, and indeed, through working with angels daily, many of us can become clair-*audient* and even be able to channel from angels, though I would stress, I always advise this needs to be done safely from within one's heart space.

In my own case, in 1999, when I asked the angels in meditation how I could tell others they were there, as I couldn't "see" them, I was guided to read certain books about sacred sound and numerology for manifesting energy. Then I learnt about the Universal "taking and giving hands" and sensitivity of our palms. Most importantly of all, I learnt about loving will and intention. It was angels who taught me clairsentience: to "feel" and "sense" their energy, first on my palms and fingers. Also, I learnt to "hear" their words whilst my consciousness was in my heart. Which brings me to the most vital point in working with the angels, which is learning to feel and sense with the heart. The more you realise this, the deeper will be your angelic connection. All (That Exists) is comprised entirely of energy – a form of Light – it exists eternally, and can never be destroyed – only changed (transmuted) into a different form. In the form of energy that is Angelic Light of the angels, we can only connect through heart, higher heart and love.

The many levels of vibration

The layers of vibration beyond what most of us see and sense are like steps. They start (at the lowest beyond our own) with ghosts and earthbound spirits. Generally these are unlucky earthbound souls or fragments of souls, remaining here through strong emotions that tie them to Earth, or souls/soul fragments associated with people who died suddenly and may not even realise they are dead. They need expert help to move on and this is rescue work done by some mediums (with their Spirit Guides) as well as humans who are Light Workers with and for the angels and Ascended Masters.

Spirit Guides are at higher levels of vibration from those earthbound entities. Having passed over, as part of their own soul's journey they have chosen to return from "beyond" to try to help the living. Guides may be people who were related to us, or they can simply have been enlightened men and women in their past lives. Either way they will be spiritually-evolved souls, often nuns, priests and priestesses, herbalists, wise women, or Native Americans and other indigenous people: highly spiritual folk who lived in synergy with Earth before being conquered by others who then forcibly introduced their own beliefs. Many of us have Spirit Guides assigned to us, and they work with mediums for readings, psychic art, etc.

On a vibration higher than Spirit Guides are pure souls called Ascended Masters. These are souls who have addressed all karma and have no need to reincarnate, but who can choose to do so to embed spiritual guidance at key times on Earth. Ascended Masters assist the angels, *St. Germain, for one, assists Melchisadec with The Violet Ray.* The Masters also help those who are incarnated now into very spiritual life paths in their soul contract like "waking up" future workers in the cause of Light, to guide their steps towards fulfillment of their soul's purpose (Soul Quest).

These are just some of the levels of vibration beyond ours (albeit some use the term, frequency, instead). Now you can begin to understand that the level of vibration goes up and up until, beyond Ascended Masters, you finally reach the highest of all: the Angelic Light healing vibrations of the angels. Then there are Three Spheres of Angels. Each of these contains three groups, so nine in all. Once we could only connect with the lowest group;

now we can access all nine. The highest of the nine are the Seraphim, Creation Angels who bring the Creator's pure Diamond Ray into our reality, where it becomes Angelic Light – White Fire; The Fire That Does Not Burn. As I have said, collectively the angelic vibration is second only to the Creator (by whatever name we call this Being: God/Goddess, Spirit, Source, Jehovah, Allah etc.). In fact the ancient texts say that this Divine Being has 72 attributes or qualities, and the angels' role is to help us work towards perfecting these qualities. That is how and why the Sacred Seven begin that journey for us. I now feel that there are144 qualities: 72 to lead us to the 5th Dimension and another 72 to attain in the 10th Dimension, but that is a story for another book...

Love, Light and angel feathers

And so to summarise: Angels can be defined as unconditional Love given form by pure Angelic Light, in other words, Essence of Love defined by and carried in Essence of Light. Their presence, and their desire to come to your immediate attention, is often manifested by the finding of a small white feather on your path, or seeing one falling in front of you as you walk, or as you are look through a window, or windscreen. It is white because this symbolises purity and Light, while a feather itself denotes the softness, warmth and enfolding power of Love. Of course it is not an *angel* feather, but if you find three white feathers in quick succession it means that they are trying to direct you towards your spiritual development. If you are reading this please look out for feathers in your own path!

Angels were depicted with feathered wings for all those reasons, even though in reality, I believe their wings are streamers of Light (as with angel-wing clouds). Having said that, when you learn to invoke them, and you detect their presence, you may well feel as if you are wrapped in thousands of soft feathers of pure Love, whilst Angelic Light fills your heart with the potential to:

- Raise your vibration closer to theirs and so detect them more easily.
- Transmute negativity within self as you begin appropriate physical healing to clear energy blocks and balance karma.
- Raise your thoughts aloft – like their white feathers – to grow spiritually.

Angelic Wing Prints

Another thing I have discovered is that when angels are in your presence their invisible Wing Print of Love and Light, directly gifted from Spirit, connects to your higher heart which is between the heart and the thymus chakras. This is detectable with training and serves as an example of As Above, So Below, linking to Hermetic Philosophy. When the angels leave your presence, this Wing Print will remain for a little while to support you, encouraging you to continue working with them, and while it remains* you are anchored on the Way of Love and Light and therefore continuously reminded of your own true worth and potential. I say this because the sad fact is that most of us do not even love ourselves... and if we cannot do this, how can we love others without judgement? *You can learn how to make this permanent.

Drawing in angelic energy towards healing and harmony

Harmony means addressing both physical and spiritual aspects of self. When the Essenes wrote of invoking angels for physical and spiritual harmony, it was because this is a way to find inner peace. Whether or not you have religious beliefs doesn't matter. Anyone can work with angels; you just need to realise there is more to life than what you can actually witness around you in a physical sense. It is true most of us can't *see*, unless we have the gift of clairvoyance, the 5th Element – Spirit, but there are many other ways to know it's there, or, we can simply trust and surrender. What we are going to do in this book is *open, and see with eye of heart* and develop your own "clair" senses into the 4th, 5th, and even, into other spiritual dimensions.

The most important thing to understand when wishing to work with angels is to strive to do this not just with mind – our left-brain gold aspect – but also at heart level – our right-brain silver aspect. I call this "seeing" and "sensing" with the "eye of the heart". The word "angels" (deriving, as mentioned previously, from "angelos" – Greek for messenger) is a most apt word. The angels – messengers of the Creator – have a role to aid mankind to develop sufficient spirituality *to see with the eye of the heart*. To work with the angels we must recognise that a higher power, what we call Source or Spirit exists and that the angels are links between Spirit and mankind. To grow spiritually instructs us to move beyond that which is visible with our normal eyes, and to bring this into balance with the eye of the heart that looks upon all with unconditional Love: Love is the only key to All.

The sacredness of seven is where All begins. In terms of Light it is seven of Melchisadec's Rainbow: your seven major chakra or energy centres, yet that is just a beginning, for with spiritual expansion comes the realisation of nine colours. Between green of heart and blue of throat comes turquoise of thymus, and higher heart of magenta (the colour of forgiveness) unlocks higher self. To appreciate turquoise and magenta they must also be sensed by eye of heart, and by doing this you make deeper connections to angels. With gold and silver, left/right-brain balance, and White Fire (sum of all colours) there are twelve Angelic Light Colours of Creation devolving from Creation's Diamond Ray.

Invoking angels and feeling/sensing their presence

When you *do* call on angels and learn how to sense their presence you are immediately making that choice, with Melchisadec, to develop spiritually as well as making the angels aware of that decision. This may or may not be a fast process, but you will instantly feel more peaceful inside and gradually less alone, because as you get to grips with developing your "clair" senses, you will know that *even if you can't see them, the angels are always there*. And while they can't take away all your issues (this is not their role), they offer you their unconditional loving support to underpin your own efforts; their role is to help you overcome your obstacles and to expand spiritual consciousness.

As I have already said, I believe angels to be pure Angelic Light rays and although they can and do appear in many forms, really they are the essence of Love and Light or "Spiritus Dei", this is Latin, meaning: the breath of God/the Creator. What we can use to invoke them are their own ancient names. The names of the angels, as recorded throughout time, carry this pure vibration embodied *within the sound itself*. Each of the Sacred Seven has a name ending in "ael" or "iel" – Hebrew for "of God". So when we pronounce the angel's name out loud this is a sacred sound carrying the healing vibration of a mini-prayer.

The first real connection you can make to a named angel is to invoke the angel from heart, using the sacred sound, and with loving intent. By this means you "call in" the Angelic Light energy – the purest vibrations that devolve in this reality from Diamond of Creation. BUT that very purity means we have to work to access it. The great thing is we can aid this by becoming clairsentient. We can learn to feel this energy on hands, within heart or crown, or simply just enfolding us, and when we've mastered this we can always move on to more sophisticated ways of connecting.

Using the Sacred Law of Three of Hermes Trismegistus

When you invoke or call in an angel, there are three golden rules: firstly, speaking the name of this being means you are utilising the sacredness of that sound. Secondly, you say the name three times. Thirdly, you must ask from heart with love.

Why call this sacred name three times? It is because of the Sacred Law of Three which *maximises* the energy we can manifest through our invocations. There are many examples of the power of three: the Religious trinities of Father, Son and Holy Spirit; Isis, Osiris, Horus; the three Magi of the Bible, all illustrate this sacred law and the power contained within it. The composition of the world: animal, vegetable and mineral: of man: carbon, oxygen, hydrogen, as well as mind, body, spirit: the measurement of time: past, present, and future, all are further demonstrations of this law in action. More importantly, perhaps, from Hermes Trismegistus/Emerald Tablets of Thoth* we learn, amongst other things, that three are the Paths of the Soul: Man, Liberty, Light.*D'Oreal 1925 translation

Making the Invocation from your heart and the angelic responses you may feel (involving one or more of the "clairs")

Let's now proceed to invoke Melchisadec. The first thing to do is to hold out your hands, palms up and relax them as much as possible. Also close your eyes. The reason for this is that sight is by far the strongest (over 70 per cent) of the five normal senses, so if your eyes are closed you can focus better on what you feel in your palms and fingers. Then all you need to do is to call Melchisadec's name (pronounced Mel-kiz-a-deck) from the heart. Ask him to be with you, using a wording which shows you are doing this with loving intent, honesty and integrity. I give you this below. *Always ensure you thank your angel afterwards.*

Say *Melchisadec, Melchisadec, Melchisadec, please be with me*
In Love and Light, Love and Light, Love and Light
Or: for my Highest Good, Highest Good, Highest Good.

Say your invocation out loud if you can, because of the sacred sound you are making, but if you are unable to do that, say it in your head, because the angels do know All. Then pause for a few minutes afterwards, keeping your hands as relaxed as possible. *Give yourself a chance to really try to feel that Angelic Light* (it is pure positive, healing energy) which will come to you in response to your invocation. If you don't feel very much, *keep practising*, it will gradually get stronger.

There are many ways of feeling and/or sensing the presence of the angels after you have invoked them, and the more you do this, the more you will feel and sense because you are developing your own clair skills.

Even if you feel nothing to begin with, which would usually be because you are new to this method, I can assure you that the angel *will be in your presence*; you must also learn to trust. In the next section I describe the usual responses that people have to this method, based on over fifteen years of working with it and teaching it.

Detecting the individual "signature" of each angel

What you are likely to feel, sense, experience, smell etc. is usually slightly different with each angel you invoke, if not at the beginning, it will subtly differ as you practise. Here are some common responses:

Touch

- The left is the "taking hand" in Universal terms, while the right is the "giving hand", *though occasionally this may be reversed, especially in left-handed people*. But you may feel one or more of the following:
- Light tickling around fingers or palms, particularly in the "taking" hand.
- Warmth on palms, along arms, heart or gently flooding your body.

- Coolness, like a soft breeze, on palms, or as above.
- Tingling like mild electricity on palms.
- Energy spiralling around hands, arms or your entire body.
- Soft, very gentle, yet strong pressure on fingers, palms, arms etc.

Sight and inner vision

- If your eyes are closed you may experience: a brief, bright flash of light in your mind.
- A glimpse of the angel or a symbolic creature, or a colour.
- When you open your eyes again you may see a sparkling in the air, or white swirling mist on the very periphery of your vision.
- There may be a subtle change in the quality of how the air looks or feels around you, tingling may then be detected on the palms.

Smell and colour glimpses

- You may detect a sudden, angelic flower fragrance that comes and goes past your nose; it can be so swift you wonder if you really smelled this scent or imagined it! Then it comes again.
- This will be a fragrance *particularly linked with angels*, such as rose, jasmine, lily, hyacinth or carnation:
  - Scents: If your eyes are closed and you smell/sense/see a flower – If the scent is like calla lily then it will be Gabriel around you, if it's a rose scent, then it is likely to be Haniel or Camael, violets would suggest Melchisadec.
  - Colours: If you "see" a sky-blue flower (e.g. iris), it links to Michael and truth, if it's a deeper blue-indigo (e.g. pansy), it links to Zadkiel and abundance or wisdom, if it's a white flower it could be Cassiel (peace, serenity) or Gabriel (hope), if it's yellow or gold in

colour it links to Raphael and healing, pink or green would associate with Haniel and heart. All these angels are of the Sacred Seven, and in this book you will learn why they may be trying to get through to you!

Sound

- You may hear tones, or some report faint booming or drumming sounds within the ear(s).

- The right ear would be associated with Raphael (he rules our left brain and right side of body), and this would be linked with healing, head, decisions and actions.

- The opposite, the left ear, associates with Gabriel (she rules right brain and left side of body), linked with heart, intuition, dreams.

What you need to do now is to practice doing this over a period of several days. Start a workbook or Angel Diary and make notes about what you felt, saw, smelled or heard, because in the next chapter, the real connections will begin.

Chapter Two

Introducing Melchisadec – Ruler of Seven & Violet

Melchisadec is the Spiritual Director of the Sacred Seven Angels and is also tasked with the spiritual fast-tracking of mankind, through his angels and powers of seven.

Symbols of Seven: Seven Rulers of the Weekdays, traditional Rainbow including Seventh Ray of Violet, Chalice of the Heart with the Key to the Seven-Turn Cretan Labyrinth

The Ancient Wisdom: Melchisadec, Prince of Spiritual Peace, Worker of Miracles, is, some might say, the greatest of all angels. In Ancient Wisdom texts, Melchisadec is "a celestial Virtue of great grace who does for heavenly angels what Christ does for mankind". The Bible tells us he incarnated as the fabled priest-king of Salem (also an ancient name for Jerusalem) and is greater than Abraham, for it was to Melchisadec that Abraham gave tithes. In the Phoenician writings Melchisadec was called, Sydik, father to the Sacred Seven Angels of the Divine Presence. In the Gnostic Book of the Great Logos, Melchisadec was Zorokothera, while Hippolytus refers to a sect called the Melchisadekians who were regarded as Heretics because they spoke of Melchisadec as being greater than Jesus, the Christ. Yet other sources speak of him as the Holy Ghost, or Prince of Peace, or even as Shem: one of the sons of Noah. The statue which adorns Chartres Cathedral, has him holding the Chalice, containing the Key, as depicted in ancient engravings, and is placed beside those of Abraham and Moses, according him equal status.

Seven is sacred within mysticism and many world religions. It is represented by the Six Point Star of Microcosm with its seventh central point. This is Melchisadec's Star. In looking over the list of meanings, it is easy to see why seven is significant in metaphysical, religious and other spiritual doctrines. In all cultures seven symbolises completeness and totality, perfection, plenty and reintegration. Examples of this significance are: ages of man, ancient wonders of the world, circles of Universe, cosmic stages, days of the week, heavens, (original) major planets of the Solar System and their associated metals, rays of the Solar Sun, musical notes. There are mystical references such as the Seven Pillars of Wisdom.

For the 21st Century: In company of his Sacred Seven, Melchisadec offers to work with you and with the Sacred Geometry and the Angelic Numerology connected with seven. Firstly he helps you towards completing a level of physical and mental healing of your first seven major chakra energy centres.

Next he tells you that the time has come for further spiritual development, guiding you to new gold and silver levels of balance in these chakras, and on opening the higher heart (eighth chakra); thus you will attain a higher level of spiritual vibration and this – the Way of Love and Light – brings you closer to the angels.

More on Melchisadec's Symbols of Sacred Seven

- His Sacred Seven Angels with whom you will work in this book.
- The Rainbow – the seven primary colour rays of healing leading to nine at the next spiritual level, and then to twelve Colours of Creation.
- The Seventh Ray – Creation Violet, used as spirals which transmute negative and dark energy. A first level of Violet is included in the Angelic Light Attunement, willed and

intended within this book.

- The Chalice containing the Key – the heart – of his Seven-Turn (Cretan) Labyrinth. This is a metaphor for physical healing as well as for spiritual nourishment, in fact it is the seven-fold path of wholeness that you can follow towards physical and spiritual balance and harmony.

When you have learned to fully access and use some of these symbols (see also the last chapter, as Melchisadec may guide you towards expanding this knowledge) you will be filled with a wonderful feeling of spiritual connection that increases the more you work with mighty Melchisadec.

Preparing to work with Melchisadec and his Sacred Seven Rulers of the Weekdays

Now that you have the background to Angelology, know how to invoke angels, and a little about Melchisadec's qualities and responsibilities, in his own words he is going to introduce himself, as well as his Sacred Seven Angels: the rulers of the weekdays. If you examine the list of the attributes, which are the focus of the Sacred Seven, and if you work with each of them, you can address most, if not all, key life issues. This will firstly be at a physical level, and then you will be encouraged to consider the spiritual aspects each of the Sacred Seven supports.

Remember the collective purpose of Melchisadec and the Sacred Seven is to aid you to self-heal in order for you to expand your spiritual consciousness. In this book you work with one angel at a time, and because of that angel's specially-designated, ancient, God-given role, this will enable you to focus on that particular aspect of your life. In the Light of his overseeing role in this, we begin and conclude this book with Melchisadec, "father" to the Sacred Seven, who is responsible for helping you and all mankind to find true self in spiritual terms.

From now onwards, if you so choose, you can call on

Melchisadec at any time to guide and support you and to fast-track your own spiritual development. Throughout the book there will be a variety of exercises to try, plus relevant channellings to digest. The material includes invocations, affirmations, meditations, visualisations and simple rituals; all are for you to try and to absorb, and I hope you will want to do this, *yet in each chapter you determine the actual focus you need.*

Note: to see colour artworks of Melchisadec and his Sacred Seven*, to help you connect visually to these mighty angels, you can also visit my website angelamcgerr.com and follow links to my Blog, e-Courses and/or informative posts on my Facebook page (angelamcgerrauthor). *Also they are included in my previously published works: A Harmony of Angels and the Harmony Angel Cards.*

For each of the Sacred Seven you can optionally add one or more of the following, to increase the energy focus you bring to your work with that angel:

Candles of appropriate colours
A dish of water, or oil burner with some relevant essential oils
crystals and/or metals linked to specific angels

Relevant information on the above will be included in each angel's chapter. However, one step at a time…for here you meet him first as Ruler of The Sacred Seven Angels. This is Melchisadec's book and by the end of it you will know him much better, for in the final section you will pull all the information together in order to work further with him. In fact you might say he can become your own personal "Spiritual Director", as he was mine for appropriately seven years *As featured in The Harmony Angel Cards, Angel Quest of the Heart, Angel Almanac.*
MELCHISADEC'S opening message:

I am Melchisadec, Prince of Peace; if you would find and keep some of my peace for yourself, I counsel you to heed my words and invoke my support, for if you seek physical and spiritual harmony, all of this and more is now possible for you..

Your world's highest and most perfect vibration is that of the angels: Angelic Light – Divine White Fire. Out of the angelic realm and via sacred geometry I descend, bringing Divine White Fire in my Chalice, and from this dazzling spectrum – the purest Light in your reality – I gently pour for you my brilliant Rainbows of healing and spiritual growth. These are the Colours of Creation, devolving from the Diamond Rays of the Seraphim, conceived in Love, carried in Light. Some of the colours are known to you, others require true spiritual perception, but since your year of 2012 the opportunities to expand consciousness with my Rainbow exist now as never before.

I am Spiritual Director to my glorious Sacred Seven Angels, yet also tasked with aiding those of you now walking your Earth who seek my help to self-heal and attain a higher spiritual vibration. This I freely offer you. If you wish to strive with me to make it so, I can clothe you in radiant Light, of all shades of Creation's Colours, that lead you back to White Fire (and even beyond to Diamond), for my role is to show you the Way of Love and Light and urge you to follow it to attain your true potential. Each colour contributes to this; therefore to bathe in my Light is to embrace my seven-fold pathway to find and fulfil that potential.

Here I manifest the power of seven for you, bringing my Rainbow, Chalice and Key: the symbols of the journey to find true self. My Chalice is filled with wonders, including the pure harmonic of each Colour of Creation in a myriad shades, all for healing and wholeness; you could call this spiritual nourishment – manna. This Light I offer you with utmost Love. My Key, enshrined within the Chalice, is another secret of Sacred Seven you may aspire to reach in due course.

First you need the seven of your traditional Rainbow, for that is how you begin to self-heal. Then, when you grow in spiritual consciousness, you will access your own higher heart. When you "see" with eye of heart; this brings perception of more colours of Creation and more aspects of each. Healing within with my Seven leads you on to Nine, then Twelve – Divine White Fire – and perhaps even to Thirteen: Diamond and Blue Star Sapphire of Earth's origins that is yet in her heart. You see, the ancient wisdom of Sacred Seven is the beginning of the path to Oneness with All.

Then there is my own Seventh Ray: Creation Violet. Because of healing work done by mankind on your Earth, more shades of Violet are accessible than ever before, with which you can transmute negativity without and within. Perhaps you wish to ask me why you could not just use Violet and heal with this, without concerning yourself with other Creation Colours. The answer is simple: nothing is gained without some effort and commitment, and self-healing (All, in fact) needs to begin at the first traditional rainbow colour: Creation Red and your root chakra and move on from there until you reach Creation Violet.

In this book, when you have learnt how to work with my Sacred Seven, you will return to me for more of my words and exercises with my Violet. By then we all hope you will have gained the wisdom and understanding to effectively channel Violet – the Seventh Ray of Mystery and Magic – and also have the will and intention to use it for All, for that is the leap in spiritual consciousness that I and my Sacred Seven aspire for you, and will always support you, to attain.

How to start?

I introduce here, and summarise the qualities of my Sacred Seven Planetary Angels who, chapter by chapter, will urge you to start healing your life with the daily support of their unconditional love. With each of them you can focus in turn on their particular key attributes, as shown below. They will support you in strengthening your strengths and aid you to overcome your weaknesses, all with a view to moving you forward towards a higher level of physical and spiritual harmony and inner peace:

Monday: Gabriel – Hopes, dreams, aspirations, intuition, Feminine energy balance

Tuesday: Camael – Courage, justice, confidence, energy, security,

> *forgiveness*

Wednesday: *Michael – Strength, protection, truth, communication, patience, calmness*

Thursday: *Zadkiel – Abundance, wisdom, kindness, integrity, humility*

Friday: *Haniel – Love, especially including of self, beauty, joy, compassion without judgement*

Saturday: *Cassiel – Overcoming challenge, peace, harmony, serenity*

Sunday: *Raphael – Energy healing and knowledge, decisions, Masculine energy balance*

Last, but by no means least, as mentioned in my introduction, remember that one of my Seven (the one ruling the day on which you were born) will be your Primary Guardian Angel and has been waiting (perhaps several of your lifetimes) for your call, please do not disappoint!

Guidance Notes

If you don't know the actual day of the week you were born on, you can find this, and therefore identify your Primary Guardian (Ruler of that day), in my book: The Angel Almanac. Also, see next chapter for more on Guardian Angels.

The Angelic Light Attunements are linked to the various Planetary Symbols. The Planetary Symbol for Melchisadec is:

Here are the Planetary Symbols for each of the Sacred Seven Angels, in the order of the chapters in this book: Moon, Mars, Mercury, Jupiter, Venus, Saturn, Sun:

Chapter Three

Melchisadec and his Sacred Seven as Guardian Angels

Of course you have heard of Guardian Angels, but did you know that in fact more than one is assigned to us at birth and others come along to guide us at certain times in our lives? And were you aware that it's not just humans who have Guardian Angels, but absolutely every single thing in the Universe? In my other books you can learn about many of these Guardians and you may decide to call on them to aid Mother Earth and All Life. For according to ancient texts there are thousands of named angels, all of whom have official Guardianship roles as laid down by the Creator and who are waiting to be invoked. This information dates back millennia, and comes from various sources, but most derives from Essene writings such as the Jubilee Scrolls, because as I mentioned before, so far as we currently have written records to access, Essenes were the first to actually document Angelology.

This is a polarity world (some say "experiment"). Therefore in the old writings there are both dark and light angels. These ancient writings tell us that when angels were created, they were all given a choice by the Creator (also said to be part of His Plan) as to which of these aspects they would espouse. The outcome was polarity. Those that chose dark became "Fallen", as of course did mankind in due course, through Eden and Atlantis. Therefore, mankind is in duality: gold (Sun) and silver (Moon) until we self-heal sufficiently (aided by angels of Light in this) to third eye chakra after which polarity can no longer exist. In crown chakra there is only Oneness and this is Redemption.

The Plan, mankind's spiritual goal, then, is to strive to transcend polarity, reach crown chakra and return to Oneness with All. In this book, we only concern ourselves with Light

Beings and how to bring Love and Light into life and I shall instruct you on how the angels aid us to begin to move through polarity and towards that Oneness. *See *Caduceus exercise in this book, also my Harmony Angel Cards, Gold & Silver Guardians, Angel Almanac*

To return to the Guardian Angels, as you will learn, the arcane sources I referred to tell us there are designated, named angels who are Guardians for the weekdays, as well as for the Zodiac Signs and all other qualities and attributes to which we aspire to make us better people. Yet also there are appointed Guardian Angels for everything around us: the infrastructure of Mother Earth, the Elements, all growing things such as the plants and trees, and for all that is needed for everything to grow and flourish. Similarly there are Guardians for all the creatures, including tame and wild animals and the same for birds. Fish and sea mammals have their own Guardians, and so do mountains and rivers, the planets in the Solar System; the seasons of the year and the Colours of Creation, in fact everything you can see around you in Earth and Sky and much, much more. When you know the names of these Guardians you can always call on them, not just for self, but to help All Life.

Back in 1999 I began to learn all this, and found that all these Guardian Angels of Love and Light have existed throughout time and all their special tasks were defined in ancient texts. We can call upon any angels ourselves for their special areas of knowledge whenever we need them, and we are urged to do this for others too. A logical starting point is with the Sacred Seven Rulers of the Weekdays. This is so for two reasons: firstly because the Sacred Seven are the Angels of the Presence, as well a being rulers of six of the Seven Heavens (Cassiel is merely the Gatekeeper of Seventh Heaven as that is the abode of God, i.e. The All). Therefore, to encourage you to strive towards these Heavens, they offer support with specific and essential human qualities such as courage, self-belief, peace and truth, beauty and love. The second reason is that of course, one of these is *your own Primary Guardian Angel*. This angel will probably have been waiting for you to take this first step, and after that, it is for you to choose how much further you go.

More about Melchisadec's Sacred Seven

Melchisadec's guidance can, as I have said, fast-track our spiritual growth, but to do this successfully you need to work first with each of his Sacred Seven because together they address all major life issues. Finally, you can work directly with him.

Here is some ancient wisdom, together with traditional correspondences for his Sacred Seven Angels: the Rulers of the Weekdays, the Seven Angels of the Divine Presence and the Rulers of the Seven Heavens. Also here I include my own modern 21st Century overviews, to help you interpret this ancient wisdom.

Monday: Gabriel, whose name means "God is my strength", is Ruler of the Moon, Primary Angel of Creation Silver, and Primary Guardian of those born on Monday. Traditionally "the Heavenly Awakener", Gabriel is the Angel of Aspirations, for Intuition, Revelation of Dreams and for the Gift of Hope. Gabriel rules the North Cardinal Point of Earth and the North Wind, although Ruhiel is Guardian of All Winds. In our current reality, Gabriel helps you to regain balance of all feminine aspects of self, regardless of the gender of your birth, and associates with the heart and emotions, imagination, feelings and hunches (see also Haniel).

Gabriel's Correspondences:
Planet   Moon
Metal   Silver
Crystals Moonstone, selenite, milky quartz

Tuesday: Camael, whose name means "he who sees God" is Ruler of Mars and traditionally the Warrior Angel of Justice. He is said, in 'The History of Magic' to personify Divine justice, courage and strength. This means power. He is the Primary Angel of the colour Red of Creation, and thus associates with the root chakra: energy, security and confidence. Yet as we see in the 21st Century, to be truly empowered you need to find forgiveness, for then you can access Magenta (Ninth Colour of Creation). Camael is Primary Guardian of those born on Tuesday.

Camael's Correspondences:
Planet   Mars
Metal   Iron
Crystals   Ruby, garnet, red agate, carnelian

Wednesday: Michael, whose name means "who is as God" is Ruler of Mercury and Guardian of the Earth. According to many arcane writings, amongst the greatest of all angels, Michael holds the fiery Sword of Light and is concerned with strength and protection, and as The Logos, he symbolises truth – both personal and the Absolute Truth of God/The Creator. We can only achieve the latter through the former, and in attaining this Michael directs us spiritually. Michael rules the East Cardinal Point of Earth and the East Wind. He is the Primary Angel of Creation Blue (different shades for different purposes) and is Primary Guardian of those born on Wednesday.

Michael's Correspondences:
Planet   Mercury
Metal   Mercury: a mirror is used as a symbol of
           the metal
Crystals   Sapphire, blue topaz, also known as Truth stones;

yellow topaz and citrine, which is a Fire stone associated with Michael's Light Sword

Thursday: Zadkiel, whose name means "covering of God". He is Angel Ruler of the Planet Jupiter, Primary Angel of Creation Indigo, Primary Guardian of those born on Thursday and listed as Ruler of Sixth Heaven. Zadkiel symbolises the spiral of Wisdom itself, and he brings Abundance, Wisdom and Integrity. He supports us to maintain our ideals and principles. As part of this, you are required to first determine exactly what abundance you need, (as opposed to what you want!) And then you must be willing to share this with others.

Zadkiel's Correspondences:

Planet	Jupiter
Metal	Tin, usually pewter is used as it is an alloy of tin and lead
Crystals	Lapis lazuli, turquoise (both wisdom stones) and sodalite

Friday: Haniel, whose name means "grace of God", is Ruler of the planet Venus and therefore concerned with gifts of life: human love, friendship, compassion, grace in the original sense, and also appreciation of beauty within and without. Primary Angel of Creation Green, Haniel also helps with healing your heart, your self-image and ability to forgive, for in order to love others you must first love and forgive yourself – see also Camael. Haniel is connected with sexuality and intimacy issues, and of course Primary Guardian of those born on her day.

Haniel's Correspondences:

Planet	Venus
Metal	Copper
Crystals	Emerald, jade, rose quartz, tourmaline, alexandrite

Saturday: Cassiel, his name means "knowledge of God". He is the Angel of Solitude and Tears: The Dark Night of the Soul. Cassiel supports us with contemplation (consideration and meditation) of our link with the Universe and Creator, something easily overlooked in our often frenetic lives. Aiding us to overcome challenges in life, as Ruler of Saturn Cassiel helps us to return to peace, harmony and serenity, reminding us, when we are really down, that the darkest time is just before dawn. He is Primary Guardian of those born on Saturday (including me!)

Cassiel's Correspondences:
Planet   Saturn
Metal   Lead, usually pewter is used as it is an alloy of lead and tin
Crystals Black and white agate, black or gold obsidian, snow-flake obsidian, jet

Sunday: Raphael, whose name means "God has healed". Raphael is the Angel of Healing and Ruler of the Sun, giver of life to mankind and all that is sentient on Earth. Raphael is said to have been tasked with healing man of his maladies and making the Earth a fit place for man to dwell. Through his sunrays that divide into the first rainbow of chakra colours (seven), he aids us, with these Colours of Creation, specifically for healing purposes. Also he offers us knowledge of energy science to help us balance the masculine aspects of self and to heal all chakras, with a special focus on the solar chakra (directly linked to him as its name suggests) for greater willpower. Raphael rules Earth's West Wind and Cardinal Point. He is Primary Guardian of those born on Sunday

Raphael's Correspondences:
Planet   Sun (regarded as a planet, although we now know it's

actually a Star)

Metal   Gold

Crystals   Clear quartz, goldstone, sunstone, diamond, citrine

Now that you have a more detailed overview of the Sacred Seven, and perhaps you have identified which one of them is your own Primary Guardian Angel, it's time to work with each one in turn.

Remember the whole point of these exercises is to gradually take you towards physical and spiritual harmony, and more inner peace, so that the more you put into this work, the greater benefit you will derive.

Chapter Four

Gabriel – Moon – Monday

KEY WORDS: HOPES, DREAMS, ASPIRATIONS, INTUITION AND FEMININE BALANCE

"I am the Angel of the Moon, darkened to be rekindled soon beneath the azure cope! Nearest to earth, it is my ray that best illumines the midnight way I bring the gift of Hope".
"The Golden Legend" – Longfellow

The Ancient Wisdom: Gabriel's name means "God is my Strength", and in old texts she is called the Heavenly Awakener. Although angels don't really have genders, Gabriel (or Gabrielle but we shall use the simpler spelling) is often thought of in female terms because the power of the Moon is considered feminine while the Sun's power is masculine. Gabriel is the angel who reveals the meaning of our dreams and supports our aspirations in life. Above all she brings us the gift of Hope. Ruler of First Heaven, Gabriel is said to have inspired Joan of Arc. To the Moslems, Gabriel (known as Jibral) dictated the Koran; to the Jews she is credited with being the adviser of Joseph and the Children of Israel; to the Christians she is Angel of Annunciation, who revealed to Mary that she would conceive and bear the baby Jesus.

For the 21st Century: How can this wonderful angel help each one of us? Firstly she supports our dreams and aspirations – it is not enough to simply have vague goals, we need to clarify them: are they *really* what we want from life? Then we must focus on them to make them happen (Raphael helps here with decisions). Consider your personal ambition and re-examine your core values. If it is money you want, how much do you need? Zadkiel, Guardian of Abundance, is more appropriate for this, although help from angels comes with responsibilities...you need to be willing to let others share in your hopes, ambitions and abundance. Or do you really want what money can buy as a way of proving your worth to others because you are uncomfortable with your self-image and dissatisfied with your life path? Perhaps you are stuck in a rut (albeit a fur-lined one!) and need a new direction. What does your intuition (Gabriel and right brain) tell you? If you answer yes to any of these questions, it is the underlying cause that really needs addressing, and therefore you need to spend time with Gabriel realistically re-assessing your life goals and planning how to attain them, while ensuring they are also in line with your soul purpose.

Gabriel and raising spiritual consciousness: reaching a higher spiritual vibration also involves balancing your Gold/Raphael and your Silver/Gabriel aspects. Gold/Solar/Raphael is your left-brain influence (right side of the body – logic, analysis, decisions and actions – what you might call masculine and head-based aspects of self. Your right-brain (governing the left side of your body) involves heart, intuition, emotions and imagination – all feminine aspects which are influenced by Silver/Lunar/Gabriel. Dreams of escape may be an expression of your right brain's subconscious feelings and you may need to bring this into your consciousness in order to refocus. All Gabriel's attributes: hopes, dreams, aspirations and feminine balance are within Gabriel's gift if you are prepared to work with her and ask for help in interpreting what you intuit as well as building and balancing your intuitive side. Remember that the objective of working with angels every day is to reach a state of physical and spiritual harmony and to move from third eye polarity towards crown chakra. Here is your chance to invoke and work with Gabriel to heal, ground and balance your feminine energy aspects to third eye, and later in the book, you can do the same with Gold and left brain: the masculine focus of Raphael, more prevalent in the world today .

In Raphael's Chapter you will learn more about the Caduceus and why working towards Gold/Silver balance in the first six chakras is important if you wish to move towards the seventh: the crown chakra, thus achieving that spiritual harmony and Oneness with All. Melchisadec and all his angels offer support to enable you to do this, realising that to be able to focus on spirituality, you need that physical life harmony also. Basically it is a double learning curve; we are determining here to first understand, then experience.

To summarise therefore, we begin the Rulers of the Weekdays with Gabriel, and with her support you need never lose hope for the future or be without aspirations or physical and spiritual life goals. Although Gabriel rules Monday, you can ask for her assistance at any time, but Monday is particularly good, because it carries extra energy focus towards this angel.

To further aid focus with Gabriel on Mondays: you can add colours, crystals and the four Elements:

- A white or silver candle for the Element of Fire, the colour is for Gabriel's Silver of Creation
- A moonstone, pearl or a piece of selenite; these are all Gabriel crystals, and also represent the Element of Earth
- Almond, hazel or lily, flowers, twigs, oil or essence, for the Elements of Air and Water

Gabriel's colour is Creation Silver and of course, her metal is silver, so you could hold or wear something silver, again for extra focus. If it's a ring or bracelet, wearing it *on the left hand or wrist (or ankle)* reminds you that it derives from right brain, which means it is the left side of you that you are focusing on balancing. (Remember that gold is left-brain, yet right side, and silver is the opposite).

First steps in working with Gabriel

Try invoking Gabriel, by saying:

- *Gabriel, Gabriel, Gabriel, please be with me in Love and Light, Love and Light, Love and Light.*
- Gabriel's energy is often felt as a cool breeze around fingers or hands or along arms, though your own response may be different. Keep practising until you feel you can recognise the "signature" made by Gabriel's energy. Do this at the beginning of each chapter so that you begin to detect the difference in each angel's energy, and your own series of signatures.

Then get started with Gabriel on the Creator's attributes that she brings you and that you need to address in yourself. Also remember the angels are here to help and support us, *so long as what we are asking for is for our Highest Good.*

Guidance is given in this chapter on how to receive your connective Angelic Light Attunement. I suggest the exercise for building your intuition is suitable for this. When you have "downloaded "Gabriel's Moon Attunement your connection (and your response when invoking Gabriel) should gradually strengthen; keep working this and be patient. As mentioned before, there are no "quick fixes" if you are going to commit to doing this properly.

Gabriel opens her chapter by saying: *My key words are* **HOPES, DREAMS, ASPIRATIONS, INTUITION AND FEMININE**

BALANCE, *please consider which of these you need most in life, or the order in which you need to focus here.*

Now, after deciding what your focus or priority will be, try invoking Gabriel as follows:

- Gabriel, Gabriel, Gabriel please bring me new hope (*or whichever one of Gabriel's key attributes – new aspirations, goals, intuition or help to attain more Silver/feminine balance you have decided on*), in Love and Light, Love and Light, Love and Light.
- Even if you do not feel much to begin with, and I only felt a little myself at the start, *trust she comes when you call.*

Working on the key attributes: Hopes, dreams, aspirations and ambitions

Here is a focus if you need to reignite these in life. First a channelling from this angel, specifically if you need to be aided with new hope and/or aspirations after bereavement, rejection, loss of job, poor health or depression.

I, Gabriel, come to you in your time of difficulty and hardship. I bring you the Creator's gift of hope to support you in determining a new goal or aspiration to which you can work, for when you have dreams and ambitions you have the motivation and energy to work towards them, but when you lose your dreams and hopes you may feel bereft and despairing. Perhaps you will catch the scent of the calla lily and know I am with you, or you may feel the warmth of my gentle energy around your heart or hands. Even if you don't yet feel this, when you call me I enfold you in my wings of clear Silver Light to show you a new dawn.

Whether it has been the bleakest of times, or even just a severe setback, my gift of hope empowers your new beginnings. Just as the snowdrop heralds spring, so I come to bring you the possibility of a better future. If you need a completely new start, cease to make compar-

isons with your old life, for aspects of your old self need to be discarded; it's time to move on. I invite you to open to my message of hope and as I bathe you with Silver radiance, I help you to heal with my unconditional Love. With me and my fellow angels of the Sacred Seven you can really begin to heal your frozen heart and regain your balance in life, once again feeling ready to greet the Light.

Affirmations are a simple way to begin

Here is an Affirmation you can make with Gabriel to begin to build new aspirations. You can use this either just on Mondays or as often as you feel it is necessary. Write it down for yourself, change the words if you wish, put it up where you can see it and when you say the words put as much energy into it as possible. Keep doing this until you feel your goals taking shape, and things beginning to change.

For a new goal or aspiration in life: *Gabriel I thank you for your loving support and for your help to re-kindle hope in my heart. I empower my intuition with you and re-focus on my aspirations. Help me to listen to heart, using my enhanced intuition to understand how to pursue my own way forward, as I seek a new goal for my own Highest Good.*

Many of the hopes, dreams and aspirations we have are about relationships.

Gabriel offers aid for love issues (see also Haniel's chapter). Are you contemplating a relationship or attracted to someone and need help from Gabriel? But is this for your Highest Good? Find out by invoking the angel and saying:

- Gabriel, Gabriel, Gabriel, please bring your Silver moon rays to me to guide my hopes and dreams over (name), so long as this is for my Highest Good. (*Later in this chapter there is a meditation for you to try.)*

You can also try "scrying" with Gabriel in order to gain an intuitive flash or angelic glimpse. You would do this to enable you to "see, hear or sense" (your "clair skills") or so that you would be able to dream something that is specifically connected with ambitions you might hold in terms of a relationship or a new venture.

- Take a shallow round bowl of clean water and place a small moonstone or milky quartz crystal in it; the crystal needs to be fully submerged.
- Put the bowl where moonlight will shine on it for 28 days of a Moon Cycle, or if that is not possible, over one full night (Full Moon is best of all) to energise the water and crystal with Gabriel's energy.
- The next evening (in moonlight if possible) say, *Gabriel, Gabriel, Gabriel, please show me what I need to see, or guide me, for my Highest Good.*
- Breathe in Silver moon rays, hold this breath in the heart and focus your gaze into the moon-lit bowl for about 30 seconds.
- Close your eyes and "see" what you can see. N.B intuition must be/is immediate!
- *If you do not "see" or "sense" anything,* place the crystal under your pillow and mentally ask Gabriel if you can dream about your true love partner, or:
- Carry the crystal around until you meet the true person of your dreams.
- Remember to thank Gabriel for helping you.

Attaining greater feminine balance with Gabriel, regardless of birth gender!

Gabriel is the angel ruling the moon's monthly cycle, known by

41

the ancients as the 28 Mansions of the Moon. Moon energy is feminine and it therefore reinforces the feminine side of our personality. Whether we are born male or female we are each composed of these two influences: golden masculine energy (Sun/Solar influence from the left brain hemisphere which equates to your right side and right hand) and silver (Moon/Lunar, feminine influence which is from your right brain and equates to your left side/left hand).

Masculine energy gives you logical thought processes, combined with decision-making and analytical skills; this is the remit of Raphael who comes later in this book. The moon's feminine energy is mainly vested in the heart and thymus: seats of our emotions. Silver actually develops your intuition, imagination, and appreciation for art, music and poetry. These are subtle and emotive life influences that cannot be measured or analysed, but need to be felt and experienced. I have mentioned the first Seven Rainbow Colours (out of the Twelve Colours of Creation). When you work with Gabriel you are enhancing spiritual perception and may begin to *sense* the Creation Colours of Turquoise and Magenta; see below and also Haniel chapters).

However, to return to Gold and Silver, it is necessary to work to balance these two polarities in the correct ratio within each of the first *six* major chakras, because when you do so, you will move towards fully integrating a level of physical and spiritual balance from the root to the third eye *(see Caduceus symbol in Raphael's Chapter to work with this, also Harmony Cards, Gold & Silver Guardian Angels and Angel Almanac)*

The Caduceus symbol goes down into Earth, with the wings symbolising Air (both Elements ruled by Ariel). The Solar and Lunar snakes cross six times, representing the six major chakras from root to third eye, above which the wings are shown. As you learnt in the Introduction, this is a world of polarity that we incarnate into, yet when your energy centres are correctly balanced and harmonised in Solar and Lunar aspects from root up to third eye, and your heart is open, the next spiritual step is to the crown chakra and so moves out of polarity. For the sum of the colours is white signifying the transition to where duality can no longer exist. That is what the haloes of saints and angels signify…crown, Divine White Fire and Oneness with All.

To return to Gabriel, whatever you aspire to be in this lifetime, Gabriel helps with this, opening the way to understanding yourself and your true core values, so that you can build new dreams and aspirations on these, not forgetting spiritual growth. By bolstering your Silver, feminine side, and later balancing this with Gold, you will become a more rounded person. Silver enables you to be fully sensitive to the needs of others: a prerequisite of spirituality. Gabriel also helps reveal to you your potential, leading towards further clarification of your hopes and ambitions in life. To aid this task, Gabriel suggests using moonstone or selenite to gradually open your heart during a 28-day cycle, drawing down the waxing power of the magical Mansions of the Moon, or a full moon meditation.

Read this channelling from Gabriel several times to help you towards harmony and balance as it will strengthen your new aspirations. Gabriel invites you to try this simple way to breathe in and draw in Moon energy to aid your intuitive thought processes, as well as helping you to balance your silver/feminine aspects.

Mine is a pure silver spiral that flows clockwise from Mother Earth to link with my Moon, governor of your emotions and moods. I am the spiritual awakener in your dreams; that is how I bring you fresh hope and new aspirations. Yet this is not enough, for my task is to guide you to fulfil your aspirations, deal with your karmic issues and progress on the spiritual path towards greater harmony and ultimately Oneness with All.

As you now know, this firstly requires a balance between your active side (issues to address, decisions you make and corresponding actions you take) and the passive side of you (your emotions, thoughts, feelings, intuition and imagination). Raphael and the Sun govern your Gold aspect but it is I who care for the passive side of your personality with my Silver Moon rays. It is my role to encourage you to balance actions and head with intuition and heart. During an entire Moon Cycle (my 28 Mansions) you can place a crystal in a window to absorb my Silver rays. My loving guidance can be invoked on any day, although it is particularly powerful on Mondays, my own day. When you choose to do this, hold your crystal, breathe in Creation Silver; imagine drawing it through your feet in a clockwise direction and allowing it to spiral through your energy centres into your heart.

As you bring through my Silver of Creation, absorb it into each chakra, even into the cells of your body. Feel Silver rays dissolve barriers you erected around your feelings to prevent hurt. Sense your heart and intuitive skills expand, feel emotional balance being restored. Then let the energy spiral on through throat chakra towards your right brain (third eye chakra) where, later, as you work with Raphael in the same way, it will join its Silver radiance with the Golden energy of Raphael. Then breathe this radiance into your moon crystal, which can then emit this energy daily for you. You will begin to harmonise your masculine and feminine aspects and so engender a new sense of peace. If you work at this, with me and with Raphael, you can gradually attain the physical and spiritual wholeness you deserve to find the way of Love and Light, for after balancing to third eye you begin to leave duality behind and move towards Crown, Oneness and even Unity Consciousness. *See Raphael's Chapter

Building intuition (Silver) and so re-defining aspirations

If you draw on Gabriel's Silver Moon energy at a time of the full moon, you will maximise this energy potential. Expand on the previous exercise by doing this Full Moon Meditation while holding Gabriel's words in your heart.

As Ruler of the Moon, Gabriel can help you to draw on *the maximum feminine power of the full moon*; this allows you to further develop your intuition (Silver aspect). You need plenty of heart's intuition to truly re-define aspirations – to really gain understanding and realisation of your true potential. The time of most benefit from this is of course the day of a full moon itself. You could add one of the specific crystals that have already been suggested: moonstone, which is for developing inner wisdom and resources, and learning to follow your hunches, or selenite, which is named for the moon. You can also use milky quartz or angel hair quartz (a general stone). The meridian line referred to goes from the crown on top of the head, the spot where you find a baby's fontanelle, through all the major chakras.

- Invoke Gabriel by name three times, and then ask her to help you focus the powerful energy of the moon to your heart and your mind, to develop your intuition, in Love and Light, Love and Light, Love and Light.
- Ask Gabriel to completely surround you with protective pure Angelic Light during this meditation. In your mind see the radiance all around you.
- Imagine roots growing from your feet into the floor, anchoring and grounding you in the heart of Mother Earth.
- Take some slow, deep breaths in and out and focus within on the heart.
- Allow your mind to relax and go deeper. Let external sounds become part of the background, yet maintain your focus within heart.
- Visualise the meridian line within your body, extending downwards.
- Visualise the Moon and Gabriel's Creation Silver rays. Draw this silver radiance *clockwise* down into your crown: your ultimate spiritual connection to Oneness.

- Next feel the energy filling your brow (third eye), reaching your inner wisdom, the subconscious and the world of your dreams. Fill this area with Silver.
- Now it spirals clockwise down to your throat, which is your power of creative expression, empower this chakra with Silver.
- Ask for Gabriel's help to focus the powerful energy of the moon to your heart, to heal it, clarify your life purpose, build and re-empower your feminine attributes.
- You can also ask Gabriel for your Angelic Light Attunement here, to connect to her more deeply. (Even if you don't feel this, you will receive it if requested).
- Now imagine the energy flowing further down the meridian line, through solar, sacral and root chakras, until it completely fills the meridian within your body; then let it travel down your legs and softly tingle in your feet.
- Through your feet send this healing energy to the heart of Mother Earth, and ask for her blessing on your life path and new aspirations.
- Mother Earth will magnify it in gratitude for your help, and send this back into your energy meridian.
- Silver energy flows up, clockwise again, and fills the meridian; you may feel the combined powers of Earth and Moon now radiating into the seven major chakras of your body.
- Ask to understand your own true potential and for the ability to develop into it for your highest good. Feel filled with purpose and a renewed sense of direction. With Gabriel, send this energy back up to the Moon to ground you. If you can, stay a while in this sacred space. When you open your eyes remember to thank Gabriel.

Moon rules the tides so Water of Life (your emotions) is linked with Moon.

To further empower intuition when evaluating options, Gabriel weaves the Sacred Sea of your birth into Silver to boost intuitive skills and cellular healing. This final exercise helps with balance if you are too gold inclined *(gold is Sun and so linked with fire)*. Are you a Zodiac Fire Sign? If so, you may be too inclined to make snap decisions or evaluations. You will sense more when you have worked with all Sacred Seven, and determined your Gold balance with Raphael. Then you could return to do this exercise again.

- Close your eyes and start taking deep in-breaths of pure White energy, willing and intending that it is Spiritus Dei – Breath of God; breathe out any negative emotions, until you start to feel relaxed.
- Focus on the need to heal/restore your very cells (80 per cent water) and further balance your Silver (feminine – feelings, imagination and intuitive) aspects.
- Invoke Gabriel like this: *Gabriel, Gabriel, Gabriel, I ask for the power of Moon's Silver, holding Water of Life energy, to flow in to cleanse, heal and balance me, in love and light, love and light, love and light.*
- Now imagine that you can take a deep breath in of the Creation Silver power of the Moon, and that this time it is interwoven with palest aqua, Water of Life energy. Breathe this deep down into your body, firstly visualising the feminine (silver – water) energy balance being restored, balancing your emotions between throat and heart, expanding your heart.
- When you feel this balance has been attained, imagine you can breathe in, yet also breathe out, Silver woven with pale aqua.
- As you breathe out say: I breathe a Star* around me to strengthen my feminine aspects, boost powers of intuition, and guide aspirations. Help me with this, and to think

matters through before I act, ensuring I make choices for my ultimate highest good.

- You may be able to actually feel or even see this Star* energy around you! It's likely to last between 36 and 48 hours, after which you would need to do this process again, re-visualising it to re-create it.
- Do this exercise as often as you need to ask for Gabriel's loving assistance with intuition to balance your life actions and thank Gabriel for helping.

If you saw your star – what shape did you see? This could be significant in your Dance of Six and Five. Remember if you see a six-point (Macrocosm) star the angels are telling you that you need to focus on self-healing, while a five-point (Microcosm) star would corroborate that you are right to be taking the time to seek and obtain spiritual direction.

Working through the exercises should have enhanced your Silver, feminine aspects, and brought you closer to Gabriel. You can do them as many times as you like. The choices are all yours.

More Gabriel Crystals

Selenite is one of Gabriel's crystals and the name (as with the given name Selene) actually means moon. It is a beautiful translucent white, and when polished it has a vertical ray (chatoyancy) through it that can shine like moonlight itself. It is a calm, serene and pure stone, helping the user to clarify thought and develop inner consciousness. It can also be used for past life recall and psychic protection. Selenite is particularly helpful when invoking Gabriel for assistance as an alternative to moonstone, *but make sure you do not use it for scrying in a bowl of water as selenite is water-soluble!* For that use the other crystals suggested in this chapter.

Ancient Angelic Wisdom – Gabriel

The Angel of Reims

The famous "Smiling Angel" of Reims Cathedral is thought by many to be Gabriel. Although the figure's hands are now empty, they probably originally held the lily with which Gabriel is usually associated. It is interesting to note that the Fleur de Lys emblem of French royalty (and of sacred wisdom) is of course a representation of a lily. Paintings, especially Renaissance ones, also depict Gabriel holding this flower when appearing to Mary, Mother of Jesus.

Gabriel's guidance for inspiration and hope

Gabriel was believed to have appeared to Joan of Arc to inspire her to go to the aid of the French King. In WW1 Gabriel was said to have been seen by the French soldiers in the Battle of Mons, although British troops thought this apparition was St. George, see more on this in the Michael Chapter.

Chapter Five

Camael – Mars – Tuesday

KEY WORDS: COURAGE, JUSTICE, CONFIDENCE, ENERGY, SECURITY, (OFTEN FOUND THROUGH FORGIVENESS OF THE PAST)

"Even as the stone of the fruit must break, that its heart may stand in the sun, so must you know pain"
From "The Prophet" – Khalil Gibran

The Ancient Wisdom: Camael, whose name means "He Who Sees God", represents courage combined with nobility and he has sometimes been depicted in the guise of a leopard crouching on a rock. In the 'History of Magic', written over 150 years ago, Camael is described as "a name that personifies Divine Justice". In fact some sources state that this angel goes back even further, to the mythology of the Druids. He has always been associated with Mars, the Red Planet and the God of War; hence his day is Tuesday, the day of Mars. Yet Camael is one of the angels who appeared to give comfort and solace to Jesus in the Garden of Gethsemane. In the angelic hierarchy of nine groups, he is Ruler of the Powers Angels, their 11:11 Star Gate and Fifth Heaven.

For the 21st Century: Camael, then, firstly stands for justice: the righting of wrongs, or support in situations of justifiable anger in a worthwhile cause or in dealing with blocks from the past. Have you felt yourself to be the victim of a past miscarriage of justice? Even if it is relatively minor, the sense of indignation is strong and may never be entirely lost. Indeed you may have suppressed or internalised your feelings throughout your life to the detriment of your physical health as well as spiritual progress. If this resonates with you, now is the time to consider how to overcome such blocks, for if you can't change the past, *you can change your own attitude to it by invoking Camael to help you to put the past firmly behind you.*

Or do you have a battle looming right now, for fairness for self or a loved one. If this scenario resonates with you, Camael is the angel to invoke to offer strength and encouragement in aid of a just cause. Then there is the issue of courage. Many of us feel fearful at times, about life, about the future, about the world in general. This is perfectly understandable in this stressful age, but fear constricts the heart, it creates boundaries and even causes a contraction of spirit. It therefore prevents us from developing our potential in life, as well as impacting negatively on those seeking spiritual growth. Camael brings us the courage to move away from fear, letting it go so that we can remain in the heart space. If you are facing any battle he can aid with self-empowerment to enable you to establish the reality of your situation, however difficult, and having done so, can help you to find the courage, energy and determination to see it through and move on.

Camael and raising spiritual consciousness: This chapter offers ways for you to become stronger, more empowered and with secure foundations on which to build spiritually, for of course Camael and Red of Creation are linked with root chakra issues and root chakra (base of the spine) is the first of the seven (later nine) major chakra energy centres. Root connects us to Mother Earth and gives us the potential to rise to crown, though this involves forgiveness of all past issues, including forgiving yourself. Symbols associated with root chakra are a red rose, or a red cube; these all add more focus to your quest. The cube is the Platonic Solid for earth and grounding, thus giving those firm foundations, so perhaps a masculine and physical life aspect, while the pink (pale red) rose is a feminine aspect linked with forgiveness and love, often needed to clear certain root chakra blocks.

Insofar as spiritual development is concerned, as you become more used to working with Camael, and before you can fully draw a line in the sand and step over it, he will ask you to focus on forgiveness. This is something which arises in several of my chapters and basically is a key spiritual step – whether you are forgiving someone who has wronged you in the past, or sometimes even more importantly, forgiving yourself for something.

Practice invoking Camael as follows to see your response:

- *Camael, Camael, Camael, please be with me to bring courage (or another of his attributes), in Love and Light, Love and Light, Love and Light.*
- Remember to ask for your connective Attunement to Camael, using one of the pieces in this chapter. This should gradually strengthen your response.

To aid focus with Camael on Tuesdays, and to add extra energy when doing meditations, or making your affirmation, you can use:

A white or red candle (there are different reds: ruby, crimson or scarlet would be general red shades if you need energy, courage or empowerment, while you should choose magenta for any/all forgiveness issues.

Ruby, garnet or red agate, red carnelian or bloodstone (believed to be the blood of Jesus falling on green jasper) also particularly assists with fighting injustice with the power of Love and Light.

A red rose, peony or poppy (real if possible, although artificial will suffice). By looking at such with the correct will and intention you can absorb the colour.

Patchouli, angelica* or vetivert oil or essence (but always take care when using oils if pregnant).

Camael's metal is iron, so introduce a piece of iron (could be wrought iron as in a candlestick) to add even more focus.

Remember Camael aids us with root chakra issues, linked to Creation Red, but what exactly does Creation Red represent?

Red is the foundation Colour. First of the Twelve Colours of Creation, it is the passionate and fiery energy that starts from the base of your spine and powers the physical strength of your body. At the same time it is the sense of security needed to build confidence, enabling you to take day-to-day dramas in your stride. Therefore the message of the angels is to focus on red if you need help with:

- Starting off on a programme of energy and well-being with Creation Red, *(Energy/strength)*
- Putting down firm roots to increase your sense of stability and security in life, then you can build upon these roots *(Grounding/foundations)*
- Letting go of fear, with red, the colour of courage. Red energy helps to right wrongs or injustices *(Courage)*
- Unblocking your life. If it is stalled because of past hurts red is the colour to help you to find forgiveness of self or others *(Forgiveness)*
- Aiding and empowering you by building confidence, self-esteem, individuality and assertiveness *(Mental empowerment)*
- Clearing the meridian line within from root to third eye *(Spiritual progress)*

Camael says: These are my key words: COURAGE, JUSTICE, CONFIDENCE, ENERGY, SECURITY, FORGIVENESS*; *determine now which of these qualities you need. (*Forgiveness is also addressed with Haniel in her chapter on heart)*

Consider each of these key words carefully. Some are easier to address than others. It's easy to connect to Camael, to ask for and receive some energy.

- Do you need a quick energy lift? Wear a red flower! Or buy an accessory, a scarf or piece of jewellery, even underwear, and place it somewhere, or wear it, where it will be constantly in your vision to remind you to ask in your heart for Camael to help you find energy and/or that courage when you need it.

Empowering a deep desire to be original, alternative or individual

- If you feel you've been living a lie, and need Camael and courage to start to let your true self emerge, make Creation Red a major part of your life until you've made this happen. You must make the choice and the decision(s) but Camael will support you if this is part of your own self-healing.

Camael advises: *Don't be afraid to follow your own path, try to believe in yourself for I am here to give you loving support – you need only ask me to come and I shall be with you, bringing Creation Red energy and strength.*

The key attributes to work on with Camael
You could try Affirmations to increase inner confidence and/or conviction, and/or to clarify how to attain your new goals in life,

building on new ambitions and aspirations you set with Gabriel. *(NB. Vary wording to suit your own situation, but ensure you keep making the affirmation until things change)*

- For a greater sense of security: *Camael I have put the past behind me and I deserve the chance to achieve my newly determined aspirations. With your help I shall create the firm foundations I need on which to build and achieve my true potential in life.*

- For more confidence: *Camael I know that deep down I am capable of the inner confidence and conviction to live my life the way I wish. Supported by your love I shall be courageous in pursuing this aim and I shall not give up until I succeed.*

Courage, confidence, security

Harder things: Camael supports those who need to overcome the past – if your past has been difficult, and you need courage and confidence to begin to put it behind you, why not work with Camael and begin to regain some passion for life?

As I have said, Camael is the key angel for those who have been bruised and battered by circumstances. Life is not always fair, and perhaps you feel that the scales of justice have been weighted against you in the past. Maybe there were karmic reasons for this. Camael's main remit is to aid you with the courage to change your life for the better, provided this is what you truly seek in your heart. However, first you must make the decision that you cannot redress the balance with violence or anger – even bad thoughts can create more karma. Nor, if filled with fear, can you achieve spiritual development. Fear constricts your soul, preventing you from finding and fulfilling your true potential.

Love, on the other hand, hugely expands your soul and with

enough love you can truly become yourself, the person you were designed to be when the template of your life was written in the stars. You will need to try to open your heart, invoking Camael to help you find the courage for forgiveness if necessary. Exercises are provided, helping you to visualise pure Creation Red flowing into your base/root chakra, in the way that you need it, to increase your sense of security, strengthen your foundations in life and then enable you to build on them. You can ask Camael any time to be empowered with positive energy plus the loving determination to draw a line in the sands of time in order to begin again; as always, it is a matter of your choices.

Issues of injustice may or may not involve forgiveness. Either way they may be blocking the root chakra, thus holding you back in your life. If this resonates, here is a meditation for empowering you to let go of a block from the past, and/or asking for justice for someone, or assistance with courage to find or seek forgiveness. *NB: This may be the most important step you ever take to empower your own future.*

Forgiveness: often the hardest issue to tackle

Camael asks you to try to address any forgiveness issues you have, either with others or perhaps with yourself. Do you vow to resolve these issues? If so, do this visualisation *to be free to move forward spiritually.*

- If you have a red crystal (see list) you can hold or wear this as it adds more energy, though it is not essential. In the same vein, you could float two or three drops of patchouli, vetivert or myrrh in a water dish or oil burner.
- Invoke Camael for justice and courage, close your eyes and ask for his connective Angelic Light Attunement to give you extra courage.
- Optionally, also invoke Haniel (pink of love). *Haniel is covered in later chapters of this book – read about her now if*

drawn to do so and then return here.

- Breathe in the White Light that is Spiritus Dei (Breath of God), breathe out negativity, until you feel ready to go on.
- Try to visualise yourself in a cool square room of white marble.
- In the centre is a marble plinth on which, at eye level, stands a large copper bowl of leaping flames. (*Copper links to Venus and so to power of Love*).
- See that the flames are of Creation Red and you may notice sparkles of healing Gold or Silver, or pink, the higher vibration of Red, linked to heart.
- Step up to the bowl and breathe in the flames, drawing them right down to the heart. Fire of Life cleanses and purifies, reducing dark, negative energy to ash which will flow away down the meridian. Let the flames fill heart and do their work, then allow them to flow to your root chakra, while asking Camael for courage to forgive. Look within and see root chakra becoming clearer, with Creation Red of courage, radiating this back to your heart.
- Now, if you are ready, ask the Angels to bring forward and manifest in this room *the essence of anybody needing your forgiveness*, giving them a form you can recognise (*it may even be yourself*).
- Even if you don't "see" these forms, just "*know*" they're there.
- Offer your forgiveness and it is really important to mentally embrace the form(s) with Love. *You may see the Red becoming more Magenta which is a good step.*
- As you free yourself emotionally, the forms will recede into the flames, back to Light*. *This can even release trapped soul fragments: loved ones you have lost whom you are clinging to, or vice versa, allowing these to return to Light.*
- Now you can accept future gifts you are given in life, safe in the knowledge that by the power of Love and Light and

this act of forgiveness you have freed yourself from the blocks this caused and truly moved on spiritually.

- Ensure you thank all the angels involved.

Camael and Divine Justice

This is potentially a brand new beginning. To help you step further over that line in the sand, next there is a Camael channelling for you to read, to bolster confidence and determination for just outcomes in your dealings with others. Read this to see if you need Camael to let go of fears and similar negative energies.

I exemplify the Fire of Life and gilded crimson force of courage that involves passion: fighting for what you believe in, gaining the utmost from opportunities – a passion for life itself. I am Divine Justice and guide you towards your empowerment of Light. On Tuesday, my day, focus on enhancing your energy and invoke me to help you succeed in your personal battles. My Light Wings of Creation Red hold and support you as you fight with integrity and vigour for your principles, for all you have achieved, and for those you love. For if you do not have this courage, to defend all you hold dear in life, in the end you may lose everything. To stand firm in what you believe to be a just cause is not easy, as it takes conviction, perseverance and determination.

If this is what you need then the power of my Love fills you with these qualities to help you accomplish your aim, because combining love with power makes for a radiant strength that will flow forth from you and also inspire others to action. Finally I join with you to re-affirm the foundations of your own earthly life. Perhaps you have been through a period of change or instability, making you a little fearful of the future. Let my Love take the place of this fear, and fill you instead with strength and confidence. As I guide you to build further on this, sending Red of Creation to ever energise, secure and strengthen your roots, you will be empowered with my Love to go in whatever direction you choose to find your pathway onwards and upwards to Light.

Affirming your new foundations and sense of security

Having now begun to free yourself from the past, if you can identify with these justice issues that Camael mentions you can now work at healing them by replenishing root chakra energy. This next simple meditation with Camael helps you with physical energy to start revitalising your unblocked root chakra in order to strengthen your sense of security and to work towards your new goals.

- Creation Red – this colour not only brings confidence, stability and security it also helps physically with blood circulation as well as powering the strength of the body and limbs.
- Another symbol to focus on is Camael's ruby red rose. Located at the base of your spine, it symbolises grounding and firm foundations on which to build an increased sense of security.
- Visualise the rose bud within your root chakra. How does this look to you?
- If you have been able to release something that you've previously held onto, that was blocking you, "know/ intuit" the rose bud is clear and bright, emptied of negative energy, just waiting to bloom. *NB: If it is not like this, go back and do the releasing exercise once more, but this time visualising this rose bud in root chakra.*
- Now breathe in deep breaths of purest White healing energy, breathing out any and all negative emotions that you can release, until you feel filled with this pure life force energy.
- Next invoke Camael (and/or other chosen angels) and with each in-breath, ask for Creation Red's ruby light to flow into your root chakra, filling you with glowing energy.
- *Feel* it flowing in and the process beginning to strengthen

your very foundations in life so that you will now be able to build firmly on them.

- Now visualise the rose of your root chakra blooming; it is fully open and radiating with bright, strong Creation Red.
- *Will* Creation Red to shine throughout the area of base of spine, expanding your feeling of confidence; the more you can do this the more effective it will be.
- Send it down to Earth, to ground you and to help Mother Earth herself.
- As she returns it to you, ask Camael to empower you with the specific shade you need to help you attain the new goals that Gabriel helped you with.
- Keep breathing out this shade of Red, until you surround yourself with an aura in the shape of Creation Red Light Wings this signifies to the Universe to take note: you are energised and ready for action!
- Ask to receive guidance on new goals you are ready to pursue.
- Remember to always send thanks and love to all the angels you invoke.

Camael explains further about Creation Red: *You will now understand my message is of Red of Creation. Red is for courage and stamina, power and strength. This is the colour of blood and your physical wellbeing, yet it is also the spiritual starting point. Invoke me for power of radiant crimson, like my vibrant summer roses, to energise your mind or body, and breathe bright rays into the lower part of you that needs this vitality. I support you so that you will then move on with me towards paler, higher vibrations, such as pink shades, as well as to gradually work towards other Colours of Creation. Truly this is just the start of re-empowering yourself. In later chapters you will be able to build on this new beginning.*

Camael continues: *Now re-consider my key attributes of Courage,*

Strength, Confidence, Energy, Security and Forgiveness, as by now you have worked quite a bit on these, and your intuition (boosted by Gabriel) can help you to determine if you still need help with any of them. Do you feel you have moved on? If so, I am delighted. Or, looking at it another way, it may be that that the work you have done so far enables you to go back and work at a higher level on these issues, furthering your Dance of Six; there are many levels to healing. Each level then leads to a new potential Dance of Five (see Melchisadec's chapter for more on progressing your Dance).

Our task as the Sacred Seven is to enable you to cleanse and unblock some major chakras sufficiently to begin opening the higher heart flower; this truly means you have healed physically and balanced to the appropriate spiritual level to begin to move from Sacred Seven towards Nine, yet I remind you now: All begins with me.

As you now know, forgiveness – especially of self, is vital. With Gabriel you began to work on your emotions and heart. With Camael you released key chakra blocks. This continues with Michael, Ruler of Wednesday, so that when you reach Haniel you will move further forward to healing the heart and begin to open your higher heart flower. Remember, however, that with healing you *must* start with the first chakra which is root chakra : Camael's key attributes and Creation Red are hugely important for Red is the foundation, linking you to Earth; 111 is Angelic Numerology for pure energy.

Camael offers this final message to you: *You are very dear to me, and whether you "see" me or not I am always here to offer my loving support. I wish you to know that if you have confidence in self, and are really empowered in your root chakra, there is very little you cannot achieve. As you have now learnt, it all begins with leaving behind anything unfortunate in the past and building new security and inner strength: firm foundations on which I support you to build a more harmonious future with courage and confidence.*

You have made great strides, healing to a new level. As you heal your root chakra with Red your spiritual development progresses and you will begin to see subtle variations of shades: ruby, crimson, scarlet— even, perhaps, the higher vibration that is pink. Later in this book, as you also perceive your own Truth (with Michael), you will begin to open your heart flower of unconditional love with Haniel. Though the heart flower begins as a pink lily or lotus, when you reach a certain spiritual point, having worked more with Melchisadec's Rainbow, and once Raphael has helped you heal all your major chakras, you can open the heart further with Sacred Nine. Then the flower will become Magenta of Creation, and if you attain heart Ascension, be transformed by the angels into a Diamond Seed of Life as pictured here. This is the six-petal sacred geometry flower that is the heart of the Flower of Life,

and this "blooms" at the heart of Mother Earth herself. When you remember to send healing to the Mother she helps to open and clear your energy meridian further, from root to heart: truly empowering higher heart. At a certain point, if you have pledged to work for All, and can hold this vibration, Melchisadec and other angels can gift you the Seed of Life; this is called Awakening the Crystalline Heart*: it is the first pure harmonic healing fractal; it brings new enlightenment in the form of Heart Ascension, which takes you much further on the Way of Love and Light. You will "see" and "know" with eye of heart when you are ready for this step.

*See website angelamcgerr.com for more on Awakening the Crystalline Heart.

Each and every one of us has some root chakra and forgiveness issues to address and associated blocks to release. And how can you build a new life or grow spiritually without firm foundations? Or build on these without being empowered in your lower self?

When you've read through the whole of this chapter and worked through it, if necessary, take decisions on where to start changing your life. Use the intuition you enhanced with Gabriel to balance what your head is telling you to do, and take courageous decisions accordingly. Remember that the angels see all, and are only too pleased to support your endeavours but they can't make your decisions. You have been given free will; with courage you *can* make the choices you need to make. Will you choose to do this? If so, other angels will also show you the Way.

Camael's connection to the herb Angelica (Angelica Archangelica)

- The herb angelica has an angelic significance with regard to both its seeds and its stalk.
- The seeds are believed to represent the lightness of the etheric realms, and the fragrance conjures up cosmic awareness. The seeds protect thought patterns from unwelcome intrusions while allowing assistance from angels. The oil is used to encourage creativity, vision, and inspiration.
- The fragrance of the roots (linked to Camael) can draw angels closer and helps you to express a desire for spiritual expansion. The roots also represent Michael's sword, cutting through falsehood and revealing truth, allowing in the light of compassion and understanding to our deepest feelings. This can aid you to feel the forgiveness you need to move on in life. If you intuitively feel it would help, you could use a few drops in an oil burner when doing one of the meditations, to try to let these deep feelings come forth.

More Ancient Angel Wisdom

- According to the Church, the number of angels was fixed at the time of Creation. In the 14th Century the number was calculated as 301,655,722.

- Our general perception of how humanoid angels might look is influenced by medieval art and nothing like the descriptions in the Old Testament, notably Ezekiel, which speaks of four-winged, four-faced beings. Other references mention chariots (Merkabas*), wheels and dazzling light. *Merkabas are formed from the correct way of spinning the three Dimensional form of Melchisadec's Star*

Modern Angelic Wisdom – Camael

- Quartz is a powerful crystal that is excellent for healing. Rutilated quartz (Angel Hair Quartz) is a crystal with special angelic significance. It is clear quartz crystal with inclusions of fine needles of rutile. These often look like angel hair that is trapped within the crystal, making it appropriate to use with any angel meditation and giving rise to its nickname.
- A more modern perception is that angels, who are pure spirit, manifest as coloured light containing sacred geometric symbols such as triangles, squares or circles, sometimes superimposed upon each other. Camael's energy is often very warm and heavy, but of course it may be different for you! You may see or sense Red of Creation around or flowing through you. It's important to note that the *shade of red* you see could indicate the type of healing you need to prioritise: yellow reds mean strength and/or empowerment, bluer reds are about forgiveness issues, pink links to heart healing and opening.
- The way you personally "see/feel/sense" Camael's energy will always be your "clair" signature for him, so that you know whenever he is around you. Practise your invocation so that you know exactly when Camael is with you; then at times of need you will only have to think of him, or say his name once to find that his energy swirls around you.

Chapter Six

Michael – Mercury – Wednesday

KEY WORDS: TRUTH, PATIENCE, STRENGTH, PROTECTION

"I fled Him, down the nights and down the days;
I fled Him, down the arches of the years;
I fled Him, down the labyrinthine ways
Of my own mind; and in the mist of tears
I hid from Him, and under running laughter
Up vistaed hopes, I sped; and shot precipitated,
Adown Titanic glooms of chasmed fears,
From those strong Feet that followed, followed after"
From "The Hound of Heaven" – Frances Thompson

The Ancient Wisdom: On Wednesdays we can focus particularly on Michael whose name actually means "Who is as God". He has always been considered one of the greatest of angels. Apart from being equated with St. George, Patron Saint of England, he appears in Christian, Persian, Moslem and Jewish texts. Ruler of Fourth Heaven, and Mercury, he is the Carrier of the Sword of Light, and thus he is the Chief Warrior against Darkness. He is also described as The Logos (the Word of the Creator). In the poignant poem extract above it illustrates how many of us spend years fleeing from Truth, yet those strong Feet of the loyal Hound of Heaven follow, with unconditional Love, hoping to bring us to Light.

For the 21st Century: As with all angels, support comes at many vibrational levels. Michael firstly represents strength in mind, body and spirit, and brings rescue to us in the form of his Light Sword. This helps us to start to cut away fear and other negative emotions within us in order to allow positive, blue, energy to flow in to higher self, engendering a feeling of wellbeing coupled with protection. The crystals for Michael are sapphire, other blue crystals and there is yellow topaz (for the Sword). The blue stones tend to be for peacefulness, healing and preventing recurrence of health problems, the golden stones are for initiating positive action to improve channels of communication and transforming or expanding life's possibilities.

Michael and raising spiritual consciousness: At higher spiritual levels, the Word represents Truth in all its guises, from personal to Absolute: we begin by being willing to hear truth about us, by choosing truth in our dealings with others, and through presenting our own truth to the world as well as by being loyal to our principles (here he links with Zadkiel, Ruler of Jupiter, Thursday and Creation Indigo). In all these truths, which are vested in the throat chakra, Michael helps us with timely and appropriate communication. This can be from simplest to deepest level; in fact he urges us to commence with hearing and speaking our personal truth, so that we can move forwards spiritually towards Absolute (the Creator's) Truth. In this regard his Light Sword shows us the way through falsehood. And he also brings the gift of patience and calmness – a precious attribute indeed in today's world!

As you will learn in his chapter, Michael brings various Creation Blue colours, from sky-blue to cobalt-blue and midnight-blue, according to our need. Sky-blue is generally the first blue we would associate with the throat chakra, while the cobalt is the colour of Michael's wonderful protective cloak and midnight-blue is for calmness and patience.

Michael says: *My Key Words are:* **TRUTH AND ALL TYPES OF COMMUNICATION, PATIENCE, STRENGTH, PROTECTION;** *I bring you any or all of these, with utmost Love, whenever you call me, plus my Sword of Fire.*

To aid focus with Michael on Wednesdays, you can use:

- A blue candle – any shade of blue will do as Michael has many (though Indigo is Zadkiel's Creation Colour).
- Crystals of blue topaz or sapphire, or, if you prefer, other blue stones of your choice may be held (use the left/taking hand). Michael's stones can be many shades of blue, from sky to cobalt or navy blue.
- Oils for the throat area include camomile to aid communication of truth, or cypress.
- Michael's metal is mercury, traditionally associated with the silver metal behind the glass of a mirror. You can also place crystals on a mirror at any time, to include Michael in any healing you are asking for. *This brings even greater energy focus, as the effect of the mirror is to double the energy.*

To invoke Michael and become used to feeling his strong yet gentle energy, say:

- Michael, Michael, Michael, I ask for your guidance to find my truth (or strength, or protection, (*or any other of his attributes if you need them*), in Love and Light, Love and Light, Love and Light.

Perhaps most importantly of all, having chosen to address your personal truth, and release unwanted aspects of yourself with his help and his wonderful Light Sword, (covered in this chapter) you are putting your life into greater Divine order; you can become spiritually stronger. Michael assists you to develop new spiritual awareness, and to connect with the Cosmos in a positive way (this continues with Cassiel). From addressing your own truth with him, you move towards the Creator's Absolute Truth and Oneness with All.

The key qualities with which Michael specifically aids us

Michael is an Angel to call upon if:

- You need physical strength to get through the next hour, next day or week.
- You need patience and calmness to prepare for, or recover from, a difficult communication.
- You seek to tell the truth, it will be unpopular; Michael can support you with strength and help you towards clarity of thought before speaking.
- A difficult situation needs retrieval – you can ask Michael for the necessary dialogue to deal with it.
- You feel that life is suddenly dark and you are afraid. Michael can assist you to find spiritual strength and protection from negative energy.

Michael's message: *All that exists is energy; Light is All That Is. My Light Sword holds the power that shows you all levels of Truth. Do you wish you were living your truth? Call my name to aid you and always remember that Love is the Key.*

Understanding the levels of meaning in Michael's attributes

A Michael channelling to read and consider:

From the wellsprings of Light on a dazzling beam of the fiery gold of my Sword I travel to strengthen and protect you; my brilliance helps dispel all darkness and falsehood from your life. My sword Lights your way to my Creation Blues of truth and freedom.

I bring you many gifts. As Lord of Light and ruler of Mercury and Wednesday, my first gift to you is communication in truth. I ease all manner of dialogue you engage in with others, whether at work or at home. You have but to invoke my assistance for me to bring my Creation Blue energy rays to your throat chakra to build confident power of speech. My further gifts of patience and calmness support you to find the appropriate time, as well as helping with the words you choose. For I urge you to say what you really think, and feel, perhaps for the very first time, in the cause of speaking your personal truth. Aided by my loving strength, you can also begin the difficult step of hearing and accepting the truth about yourself, and move from there towards living a more honest and fulfilled life, a life which lets go of pretence and pretension.

Also you can invoke me to bring my Light Sword, to cut away things within your life you wish to be rid of, so long as you act always with integrity, for as I remind you, the Fire of Life energy of my Sword may only be used in the cause of Love. You can free yourself after rejection by someone you once loved who has left you, but not in the reverse situation. Use it to remove old behavioural patterns, or cut away insecurity from within, allowing you to find full power of self-expression. Once you have freed yourself in this way, you can begin to actually live your personal truth and then seek the Creator's Truth.

Yet this is only one level of that which I bring you. For the throat chakra, when cleared of blocks, is a direct link to the first of the three spheres of angel groups. For then, if you wish to work with us and make that link continuous, your spiritual path will certainly move towards Divine Truth: Creation Blue takes you from your throat chakra to your third eye: it is the higher self path of Wisdom towards Freedom, and Oneness with All.

Affirmations with Michael

Here are three affirmations to address various communication, patience and truth issues; you can vary them as appropriate to your needs

- Knowing when to speak out. Michael aids particularly with this: Invoke Michael thus: *Michael, Michael, Michael, please bring your loving support to help me deal with this issue, to formulate the words I need, and to find the right moment to say them to avoid too much hurt. For the highest good of all concerned, in Love and Light, Love and Light, Love and Light.*
- Being more patient, calm and flexible towards others: *Michael, Michael, Michael, I know that I need to be more accepting of others' needs. Help me to have patience, to be calm and flexible in my own attitude to others, so they can also live their Truth. In Love and Light, Love and Light, Love and Light.*
- Living your personal truth: *Michael, Michael, Michael, I realise that lately I have been living a lie, and this is causing deep unhappiness. Please be with me now to help me find a way out of this falsehood, so that I can start living my personal truth, in Love and Light, Love and Light, Love and Light.*

Next using Michael's Sword (Light that is also the Fire of Life)
This can be used to release issues in life holding you back, or cutting certain ties that bind you, as these will be preventing harmony in your physical life and so affecting wholeness and spiritual growth.

Michael brings us his Sword of Light, as mentioned in his channelling, and this has many purposes. Use this to free you from things within that are holding back your transformation, or ties that bind you to someone or something. Perhaps a relationship has ended. The other party has walked away but you cannot forget so easily and you feel bereft as a result. If this is the reason you wish to cut these ties, you can ask Michael to help you, *but you must never use this invocation maliciously.* Your intent must remain honourable to all parties. Remember you can also cut away old mind-sets within you that prevent you from achieving your potential in life.

First you need to compile a list of issues that you wish to release from your physical life, and then, when you have done this, choose the most important one before you try Michael's releasing meditation.

To gain maximum benefit, it is worth taking the time to think about your life and what it is you *really* want to change. Do a personal SWOT (Strengths, Weaknesses, Opportunities and Threats) analysis. Take an honest look at how these affect your equilibrium. Write down your strengths and consider what they have brought into your life. Secondly write down your weaknesses, the aspects of yourself you don't like or would like Michael's help to transform. Then you can accept the opportunities that that this recognition draws forth.

You can start with physical or emotional issues. For example, you might write:

Strength: I am a good cook, and enjoy both cooking and eating.

Weakness: I overeat and under-exercise, therefore I'm overweight, and this threatens my happiness and inner peace.

Opportunity to overcome threat: *Michael, Michael, Michael, I would like to retain the strength but dispel the weakness so that I can feel myself to be more attractive to others, for my Highest Good.*

Compose your own invocation: Use it to ask Michael, during the releasing meditation, to help you cut away greediness and lack of willpower, and help you strengthen your confidence and self-discipline with regard to exercise, or:

Strength: I am a very positive individual and always try to get what I want.

Weakness: I'm too hot-tempered, get into arguments easily and don't give enough consideration to other people's feelings, with the result that my friends become irritated with me.

Opportunity to overcome threat: *Michael, Michael, Michael, I wish to retain my strength of character but release my quick tempered tendency by becoming more patient and considerate, for the Highest Good of all.*

For this issue you would ask Michael to use his sword to cut away the tendency to anger within you that flares up in these situations, and then, when you need it, help you surround yourself with relaxing, cool Creation Sky Blue energy to give you more patience, calmness and thoughtfulness.

Asking from your heart for a complete new start with Michael

When you have made your list (and remember that a complete list should address physical, mental and emotional issues that you wish to release), decide if *you really want* Michael's Sword to help release these issues and Michael's strength to support your case.

You will need to be asking for help from your heart, with a genuine desire for physical help, or spiritual development, or hopefully both. Take enough time to be completely sure about the cause of what you wish to release with Michael; there may be several issues to address so prioritise then try:

A Seven Step Meditation with Michael and his Light Sword, aided by Melchisadec and Raphael (these three together are wonderfully protective and I invoke this trinity daily around my loved ones). You can also combine this meditation with Raphael's full healing one in his chapter, or you can do this one first, and

Raphael's after that.

You have had the opportunity to make a list of issues you wish to release and you can work on them in order of priority, or tackle several at once. It does not matter whether these issues are mental, physical or emotional, if it is for your Highest Good, Michael's sword can help you to be free of them if you trust and believe in his help.

Step 1

Ensure you are comfortable, warm and undisturbed for approximately twenty to thirty minutes. Relax, detach, centre and focus within yourself. Take some deep, calming breaths, and invoke Michael to surround you with a ball of protective Creation Blue light (this would be cobalt-blue). Grow roots from your feet into the floor so that you are grounded In Mother Earth.

Step 2

Invoke Melchisadec and ask him to place an aura of Creation Violet outside the blue that surrounds you. Remember this is his Violet Ray of Magic that enables you to transmute any dark, negative energy that you have released, so that it returns to pure White Light (more on this in his chapter).

Step 3

Invoke Raphael, Angel of Healing, to place an aura of healing Creation Gold inside the blue that surrounds you. You will now be surrounded with three layers of Creation Colours: Gold, Blue and Violet, representing healing, protection and transmutation respectively.

Step 4

Open your energy chakras by visualising each as a flower in one of the Seven traditional rainbow colours (these can be any flowers really; my own suggestions are red rose, orange tiger lily, yellow sunflower, green water lily leaf and bud, blue iris, indigo-purple pansy and violet crocus*). Visualise particularly strongly the flowers in the chakras that you've identified as needing something to be either strengthened or cut away and released, see below for a guide on how to do this as effectively as possible. *Use the same flowers in Raphael's chapter.

- Put simply, indigo and violet relate to headaches, depression and mental stress issues, sky-blue is for throat problems, communication or truth issues, green is for loving relationships and healing the heart itself. Yellow is willpower, emotions, decisions, and the upper digestive tract. Orange is for the lower digestive organs, sexual and intimacy matters, and desire for change. Red is, as you know, for strength in your bones and limbs, grounding, and your sense of security.

Step 5

From your heart, invoke Michael to help you release the issues you wish to release in Love and Light, Love and Light, Love and Light. Think of your list and see the first issue in your mind's eye, place it in the flower you've pictured. Visualise the Light Sword cutting away any dark, damaged area from the flower. Feel the residue leaving your body and being transmuted into light by Melchisadec's Violet Rays that spiral continuously around you. Visualise the flower glowing more evenly. Then take the next thing you wish to address, and so on. With each issue you release, your body will feel a little bit lighter and more buoyant.

Step 6

When all the issues are released, ask Michael to bring cobalt of Creation Blue to repair and replenish any residual damage to each of the chakras concerned. Examine the chakra flowers and "see" that each one is clearer, without any dark patches, or if you can't do that, just "know" that it is!

Step 7
Now ask Raphael for Creation Gold healing for each flower; feel this being drawn down from the Sun; "see" or "know" the flower is brighter. Then request that Raphael seals each healing with his shining Gold, to safeguard the work you have done. Ensure you thank the angels for their wonderful help in this meditation, and open your eyes.

You should now definitely feel lighter in general, giving you the ability to focus directly on your powers of communication. Now it is time to make these more efficient, effective and meaningful.

A Michael Meditation for Truth: You can also use this one to download your Angelic Light Attunement. Build on the affirmations and releasing exercise by doing a simple meditation for communicating more effectively and truthfully, and optionally, ask Michael for your connective Angelic Light Attunement at this point

- Close your eyes and start taking deep breaths of pure white energy, breathing out any negative emotions, until you start to feel relaxed.
- If you have a sapphire or blue topaz, hold this in your left (taking) hand, so that you can programme it during the meditation.
- Then invoke Michael by saying
  - Michael, Michael, Michael help me to breathe your power of Creation Blue energy into my throat.
  - Having removed blocks, I need to address better, clearer, more effective communication, in Love and Light, in Love and Light, in Love and Light

- Now imagine that you are breathing in the Creation Blue that you need.
- Light fills your throat chakra and radiates around this area, dissolving any other blocks to truth, re-vitalising this chakra and helping you with greater self-expression *(in the past you may have had physical symptoms here)*.
- As this energy fills your throat, make this affirmation as well, as positively as you can, to start off your spiritual quest towards Divine Truth.
    - With power of Blue and your Light Sword, I embrace my personal truth and freedom. Please give me your connective Attunement to support my goal towards physical and spiritual harmony. *Allow a few minutes to feel this.*
- If you had a crystal you will have programmed it during this meditation. Hold it in both hands; ask Michael to seal in your resolve and thank him!
- Keep your crystal by you to remind you of what you can accomplish with this exercise; repeat it as often as you like until you find and keep your truth.

Creation Blue: Sword and Cloak for strength and protection

Michael brings different shades of blue as well as other uses of his Light Sword; this exercise with Michael contains two possible ways he can assist. Firstly you can ask for the Sword, and secondly, breathe his cobalt energy around you as a kind of Light Cloak, for strength and protection.

- If you have a Michael crystal, once again hold this in your left hand, as you can programme it during the exercise.
- Close your eyes and start taking deep breaths of pure White energy, breathing out any negative emotions, until you start to feel relaxed.

- When you feel you are ready for the next steps, you can use one or both of the following options:
  - Using the Sword to connect to the angels: Michael, Michael, Michael please allow me your Light Sword to connect to the Third Sphere of Angels for my spiritual Highest Good. (*You may well be able to "feel" this vertically through your spine or alternatively, horizontally in your hands, and it can become permanent if you are in this life to work with him*).
  - Using Blue of Creation as a protective cloak: Michael, Michael, Michael I ask for your cobalt-blue cloak of strength and protection. Help me to breathe in the power of this energy and flow it all around me, completely enfolding me, in Love and Light, Love and Light, Love and Light.
- Now as you breathe out, *will and intend* that Creation Blue spirals completely around you, forming Michael's cloak, surrounding you head to foot with cobalt-blue energy of strength and protection from negativity.
- Continue breathing and feel cobalt-blue radiating throughout your inner body, bringing Michael's energy inwards to protect each of your chakra energy centres if you feel threatened by external negativity in your life.
- Michael will help you to seal in the benefits, and also seal the crystal. Place this where you can see it every day to remind you of Michael.
- Thank Michael for his help and repeat whenever you need his protection.
- *NB: you can vary this meditation to visualise Michael's cloak around a child or any other loved one(s).*

Ancient Angelic Wisdom – Michael
- According to the Moslems, Michael (Mika'il) has emerald wings and saffron hair on his body. Each hair contains a

million faces and mouths, each one imploring the pardon of Allah.

- Ley lines are lines of electro-magnetic energy that criss-cross the earth's surface. They are believed to play a major part in the sites of stone circles and tors constructed thousands of years ago. Michael has his own Ley Line that runs from Cornwall to Suffolk, although it is fair to say that this is disputed by some. Starting off at St. Michael's Mount, it passes through, or near to stone circles on Bodmin Moor, and a succession of St. Michael Churches in Dartmoor, Somerset, Glastonbury Tor, and Stoke St. Michael. Passing by Avebury Henge, it continues to Ogbourne St. George and ends near Bury St. Edmonds Abbey. If you are ever able to, do a Michael meditation actually on his ley line to add greatly to the power, especially on a Wednesday!

- At times the Christian Church has encouraged its followers' belief in angels. In the 4th Century AD, the existence of angels was officially recognised. Later, however, the Church declared such doctrines to be idolatrous, therefore heretical and forbidden. Many angels, like Michael, were then canonised into Saints by the Church in order to make them legitimate, so to speak. So in reality St. Michael is and always has been the angel Michael.

- Some countries and cities have had Patron Angels since ancient times. Michael was chosen as Guardian Angel of Israel.

- During World War 1 (1914-18), as mentioned in the Gabriel chapter, while the Battle of Mons was being fought, a huge Light Being on a white horse is said by many to have appeared to the troops, who fell back on both sides and thus bloodshed was prevented on that day at least. It is interesting to note, from the contemporary reports that to the British troops the angel appeared to be St. George, while the Germans believed they had seen the angel Michael and the French felt the angel was Gabriel; Gabriel had been the guide for Joan of Arc.

Chapter Seven

Zadkiel – Jupiter – Thursday

4

KEY WORDS: ABUNDANCE, WISDOM, KINDNESS, INTEGRITY, HUMILITY

"In great humility, fill thy heart with the love of God; thou shalt then have a pure spirit which will grant (by the Lord's permission) thy desires. Therefore seek for that which is good; avoid all evil either in thought, word or action; pray to God to fill thee with wisdom, and then thou shalt reap an abundant harvest"
Trithemius's Book of Secrets, c1800

The Ancient Wisdom: Zadkiel, whose name means "Righteousness of God", is Ruler of the Sixth of the Seven Heavens, the planet Jupiter, and is Chief of the angelic order of Dominions. In our dealings with others he brings thoughtfulness and mercy (he is said to be the unnamed angel mentioned in the Bible who stopped Abraham's hand when he was about to sacrifice his son, Isaac). His main crystals are lapis lazuli or turquoise. Lapis lazuli, also called "the Eye of the Gods", has been revered for thousands of years as representative of the mysterious starry heavens. It was, and is believed to carry the means to acquire knowledge and magical powers. Turquoise is another ancient stone traditionally associated with the Native Americans; it signifies courage, action and most of all, wisdom.

For the 21st Century: Zadkiel holds the keys of wisdom and abundance (both spiritual and material or physical) and can help us to expand our horizons of possibility in all sorts of ways. In our physical world one of these ways is in terms of personal development, where he supports us with opportunities for knowledge and with memory – two most useful assets for success! Zadkiel brings joyful Jupiter abundance, tempered, however, with responsibility and integrity.

Yet, there are many kinds of abundance, including money, love, health, happiness and spirituality. Which do you seek? Are you prepared to share it with others? He asks that you always remember the saying: "Do as you would be done by". In other words, consider the effect of *every* action that you take and whether you yourself would like to be in receipt of such action. Are you mindful enough of this? The law of Karma tells us that any actions we take which are good, even if anonymous, will result in manifold good deeds coming our way, while those of dark intent will rebound on us threefold (the threefold return) – either in this lifetime or the next! Another key responsibility of Zadkiel's is to help us to retain our principles. So often we have to accept compromise in order to maintain happy relationships. However, we should not settle for that if it means the total sacrificing of our personal ideals, for if we do this we are unlikely to achieve long-term happiness. Therefore, remember to retain some of your youthful wisdom and idealism, even when it seems much easier to let go, avoid opposition and opt for a quieter life. This may simply be a kind of test of your own resolve and spiritual integrity.

Raising spiritual consciousness: After you have given full consideration to your abundance needs vis-a-vis personal and career objectives (and hopefully you thought about these while working with others of the Sacred Seven) now ask yourself about any abundance you already have. Even more importantly, do you recognise your own opportunities when they arise?

So often abundance is simply thought of as money, but you must also consider other abundance now, especially spiritual abundance which will help you towards that inner peace and harmony. By now, if you've worked diligently with the first three of the Sacred Seven, you will be seeing, through the attributes they bring you, a much larger picture depicting yourself and your life. Especially if with each of the angels you focused firstly on the physical harmony aspects of life, and then followed their guidance to move on to the spiritual aspects (and remember you can go back and do it all again, as many times as you like, resetting your aspirations from physical life goals to spiritual ones). It's the same with abundance. You are urged to really think about the type (or types) of abundance you seek or what it is you actually need. What has brought you to buy this book, and are you committing to working with angels every day? If so, then your path will unfold as mine did along their Way of Love & Light.

The aspect of Zadkiel that raises spiritual consciousness in a major way is Wisdom...abundance of Wisdom. Zadkiel reminds you that by adding experience to knowledge, you acquire true wisdom and that aiding you with this is his special remit from the Creator. The suggested crystals, particularly Lapis lazuli (Eye of the Gods) and mysterious turquoise, help you to be wise, but remember to always retain your principles even though life tests you; remember the angels see all. If you are an ancient soul you will resonate with this, and working with Zadkiel enables you to begin to retrieve your own ancient wisdom; it's buried deep in your heart and soul, and now you are urged to bring it forth. Wisdom links to the Sacred Geometry spiral that is Fibonacci. My first artwork for Zadkiel *(See angelamcgerr.com, A Harmony of Angels and Harmony Angel Cards)* depicts the Fibonacci spiral that underpins All That Is, as well as conveying Heaven and Earth's mirror images: As Above, so Below, as Below, so Above. Take this opportunity to consider yourself in mind, body and spirit terms, as well as physical and spiritual harmony and balance.

Now become used to invoking Zadkiel as follows:

- Zadkiel, Zadkiel, Zadkiel, I ask for your aid to find the wisdom I need (or abundance or success, or whatever other attribute of Zadkiel you need) pledging that I will share with others, in Love and Light, Love and Light, Love and Light.

- You can ask Zadkiel for his part of the connective Attunement here, or choose one of the pieces in this chapter, go into heart and ask for it.

Zadkiel tells you: *My Key Words are:* **ABUNDANCE (ALL), WISDOM, KINDNESS, INTEGRITY, HUMILITY**, *and to add energy and aid focus with me on any or all of these you can use:*

Candles of turquoise, indigo blue are appropriate for Zadkiel.

Apart from lapis lazuli and turquoise stones, the crystals already mentioned, crysocholla is also a crystal that can be used when working with Zadkiel.

Peppermint, petitgrain, basil or cypress are the essential oils to try in your burner to further raise energy vibration, *but always take care about which oils you use if you are (or think you may be) pregnant.*

Zadkiel's metal is tin, more usually found as a component of pewter (tin and lead), so use something made of pewter, like a little pewter bowl, to add even more focus.

Now that you have worked with Gabriel, Camael and Michael, begin by re-evaluating where you currently are with self and life. As I have said, Zadkiel brings all kinds of abundance into your life, but he reminds you that by accepting his gifts, it is important to ask for the wisdom and kindness to use them lovingly. We all need some abundance, *but it is for you to decide exactly what to seek.* Zadkiel says that when you determine the abundance that is top of your list you can make an Affirmation to send to the Universe, but do you have a simple request? And is your abundance request linked to a true heart's desire in this life path; one that conforms to your soul purpose? Later in this chapter Zadkiel offers his assistance with abundance requests.

Also, the angels ask you to please ensure your request is both reasonable and specific, that you set some time limits (as outside this reality time is non-linear), and that you ask for something for the Highest Good and to harm none. You must then trust it to happen. It is very important to *pledge*, as part of your Affirmation, that when your request is granted you share your abundance. Abundance of loving kindness and integrity are the tacit agreement you make when working with angels, especially with Zadkiel.

Zadkiel also assists in a general way in life with memory issues, and helps by combining this with his aspect of abundance of luck and success in exams or career moves. This expands your horizons of possibility, enabling you to gather knowledge.

Time, therefore, to determine the specific abundance that dovetails with your new priorities, and you could start with an appropriate Abundance Affirmation.

Some simple Abundance Affirmations
Based on these, you can design one that is appropriate for your needs, and make it daily until things change

To affirm your need for abundance of opportunity: *With Zadkiel I affirm my need for abundance of opportunity to fulfil my life's potential. I deserve to succeed in my quest to find and achieve my new aspirations for my highest good, undertaking to share any wealth created with others.*

If this doesn't quite fit your own circumstances, then add another angel and vary the affirmation, by building on what you have learnt.

With Zadkiel and Haniel I affirm my need for abundance of love; I deserve to succeed in my quest to find and keep the right life partner, and to be able to give and receive love, for my Highest Good.

With Zadkiel and Michael I affirm my need for abundance of support in beginning to live my personal truth. My spiritual quest is to move through personal truth towards Absolute Truth, in love and light, love and light, love and light.

Add Gabriel to seek abundance of aspiration or intuition, or go back to that chapter and add Zadkiel; same for Camael for abundance of courage and empowerment; health issues would be Raphael, see chapter ten.

If you need abundance of change, here is a Five-Point Plan to follow with Zadkiel, involving self-coaching to aid your focus on your new abundance goal(s). If your need for abundance of change is really deep, and if you identified new goals with Gabriel, Camael and Michael, then this is a real chance to pursue them, as they may well include references to abundance of one kind or another.

1   Think about your life. Determine the most important long-term goal that you need or want to achieve that will increase your feelings of happiness and abundance. Bring this goal to the forefront of your mind.

2   Now consider why you have been putting off attempting to reach this goal. What is actually stopping you from doing it? There are obviously reasons or else you would be on your way! Invoke Zadkiel to help you with the wisdom to list on a piece of paper *anything that is stopping you* from

proceeding towards your goal.

3　Now that you have identified what is stopping you from doing what needs to be done, prioritise them and then think about how you could deal with each of these inhibitors and make a step-by-step action plan. Tick off each step as you achieve it. If the list seems insurmountable, break it down into smaller goals and then do this exercise with each goal. For this, ask the relevant angels to help you with these steps – Gabriel for realistic aspirations, Raphael for health, Michael for communication and strength, Cassiel to overcome sorrow or a dark spell in life, Camael for energy and self-empowerment, Haniel for issues connected with love.

4　You have worked out, with the help of your angels, what you *could do* to achieve this designated goal in your life. Now make a decision about *when you will take the first step.* Set a date for this (or it will not happen!) It's all up to you because you are the only person who can address this, and yet the decision is yours!

5　All that remains is to make a start, and by doing so to become part of the abundant flow of the Universe (go with the flow!).

If you worked through the Plan, use your priority goal, or if not, use the abundance needs you determined earlier on; these could reflect your physical life needs. Alternatively, read the next channelling about Abundance of Wisdom: a more spiritual Abundance Request.

Whatever you decide, the next step is to frame a Universal/Cosmic Affirmation, or use and or adapt the example I give in this chapter, and then ask the angels for help to convey this to the Universe on your behalf.

This is a deeper Zadkiel channelling on Wisdom

Read and reflect on this first, and then you can use it to ask for your Zadkiel Attunement. I suggest you read it through three times, close your eyes and ask to be given your connection through the third eye chakra; then all you need to do is trust that this will happen.

Mine is the golden Light of Wisdom that flows in an infinite spiral of Divine proportion* through all Creation. Carrying abundance of knowledge and opportunity it circles continuously, at many levels, around the third eye and Indigo. Through lapis lazuli, my Indigo Gold indicates wisdom's mysterious depths. Yet abundance contains many shades, depending on what you actually need. Abundance of all kinds can flow to you with my assistance, including opportunity, intelligence and generosity, for if invoked I can guide your prospects for success, so long as it's for your Highest Good and if I know that in due course you will share your abundance with others, for in this very sharing you will benefit as much as they from the synergy of Love and Light.

Your strength of character in the past, your idealism and refusal to compromise your principles has set standards that others envy. But things are not always as straightforward as you would wish, and you may have lately wondered if you were mistaken in your view of right and wrong. Your vision is not flawed but your beliefs may have been tested. Let them withstand these tests and emerge stronger, yet refined, like gold tempered in a fire. Be reassured – there is a great deal in your personality that people admire, not least your integrity, steadfastness and willingness to share your blessings. Invoke me whenever you wish my rays of warm and loving energy to flow in to support your life and your surroundings.

My rays also help you to retrieve your own ancient wisdom, for you have the means of great potential achievement in your life. You have *forgotten much that once you knew, but as you work with me, you will slowly retrace your path on my pure Golden Wisdom Spiral. When your heart, linked with the third eye and crown, remembers All, you will understand that Wisdom has no beginning and no end, for in its end is its beginning – this realisation leads to your understanding of As Above, So Below, As Below, So Above. *Zadkiel speaks of the Fibonacci spiral and the Golden Mean.*

How to programme an abundance crystal

Do this to aid your quest for abundance and you can even hold your connective Attunement within it to remind yourself about it.

- Use any one of Zadkiel's crystals - Hold it in your left (taking) hand, and close your eyes.
- Picture in your mind the abundance you seek for your highest good.
- Raise your left hand (with the crystal).
- Then say Zadkiel, Zadkiel, Zadkiel: I ask to connect through Love to your Light and to draw down the power of Creation Indigo, threaded with your Golden Wisdom Spiral, into this crystal, to programme it for my quest for abundance.
- Help me to make the right decisions regarding the next life-changing step I can take to bring about this abundance.
- I pledge to share what I receive for the Highest Good of All.
- Now still your mind for a few seconds, and go into your heart.
- You will feel the energy flow into you and through to your hand and crystal and down to your heart.
- Raise your right hand and send love and thanks from your heart spiralling back to Zadkiel.
- Lower your right hand and place it over your left (with the crystal), asking to seal in the programming with Love and Light.

- You have programmed the crystal. Keep it near you and whenever you look at it let it strengthen and build your connection to Zadkiel while also providing positive focus for your abundance quest or quests.

Creating and sending Abundance Affirmations

Here is an example of a very general Cosmic Abundance Affirmation which is for harmony and balance relating to physical, material and spiritual abundance. If you use this one, you need to also express a time limit, because beyond this reality, in the realm of angels and other Light Beings, time is non-linear, and not as we see it.

You can use this Cosmic Affirmation, adapt it, or write your own. When you are clear about what you want, turn to the next exercise to do your Ritual for the abundance that you need. The Ritual adds much positive energy.

"I stand four-square, grounded and safe, with Gabriel, Uriel, Michael and Raphael*, and with their help I open my heart to radiate Love and Light to All That Is. Breath of Life, Fire of Life and Water of Life nourish me and give me health. In return I channel these Key Elements to send healing to the heart of Mother Earth and All Below; as she returns this magnified energy, I send it with utmost Love to All Above. For I am part of All; the Divine Fire of Oneness is within my heart. I embrace life's passion with that Fire, and ask for Breath of Life's "inner knowing" of my own wisdom to lift my thoughts and guide me further. With Zadkiel's aid, as the River of Time that is Water of Life flows through me and I go with the flow, to let it find its true level, it will bring me abundance in various – perhaps even surprising – ways. I ask for my abundance to be granted by.....(N.B. *State your time limit request here*) Then, obeying Universal Laws, I shall give as I mean to receive as an expression of my eternal gratitude to the Creator – As Above So Below, As

Below So Above.

*The Cardinal Points Angels.

Sending your affirmation during a Zadkiel Ritual for Abundance

Now you have decided on your goal and planned your actions, plus framed your affirmation (or are using the one on the previous page), you can just close your eyes to send it, or add energy by doing this Ritual with the Angel Zadkiel and others. However, you must be completely honest in intent and ask only for your own Highest Good. Carry out the Ritual during a waxing moon, best of all, on the nearest Thursday before a full moon. Again, every action you take here adds extra focus to the Ritual.

- Start by cutting a square of indigo, turquoise, gold or white cloth or paper.
- Select a deep blue or turquoise candle for the Angel Zadkiel, etch into it the sign for the planet Jupiter (see the beginning of this chapter), and place it in the centre.
- Add a crystal for Earth and for Zadkiel, preferably lapis lazuli, or turquoise, or you could use quartz, to secure your foundations and for wisdom and prosperity.
- Add a feather, preferably white, to represent Air – Breath of Life.
- *Optional*: add crystals for Gabriel and Michael, plus Uriel (amber) and Raphael (quartz); this brings in the angels of the Four Cardinal Points and Four Winds.
- *Optional:* Use an oil burner or float on water a few drops of frankincense, to aid the spiritual purity of your quest, or one of the specific oils mentioned in this section. This also adds the element of Water of Life.
- Then, as you light the candle, Fire of Life, call on the Angel Zadkiel to assist your Abundance in the name of the planet Jupiter, and say that you wish to send your Cosmic

Affirmation for your Highest Good.

- *Next read or recite your chosen Affirmation from your heart.*
- When you have done this ask Gabriel (North), Uriel (South) Michael (East) and Raphael (West) to send their mighty Winds to hold and speed your affirmation and state your time limit for the abundance.
- *When you've done this, just ask your heart to help you let it go.* This is really important as if you keep agitating over it you may interfere with Universal action and even get in its way! There is no need to dwell on it, simply send it and then try to release it from your conscious mind for the time period you stated.
- If you can safely do so, leave your candle to burn out. If not, always snuff out candles, as you lose considerable fire energy (passion) by blowing them out.
- Remember to thank all the angels for their support and assistance.

You can use the following to alternatively download your connective attunement while you focus again on spirituality and retrieving your own ancient wisdom, for as Zadkiel reminds you:

See the nautilus shell with its beautiful geometry. Trace the spiral either way; you will always return to the same point, yet you will have grown spiritually while tracing that spiral. This is like my Spirals of Wisdom; though wisdom spirals have many dimensions, from the dawn of time to present day the Creator's Divine Wisdom does not change. It is as it always was – Divine Order in Macrocosm – All That Is.

Your own Wisdom Spiral is similar, and there are many revelations to come. Your next revelation is a point on that spiral, waiting for when the time is right for you to remember and to ground it in Microcosm – your own heart. When you receive my Attunement, I set in motion your next steps on the upward spiral of Love and Light to the Stars.

Retrieving your own ancient wisdom

Next you can try a meditation to invoke Zadkiel's help in retrieving ancient wisdom, as this is a key step in your spiritual development in this life. This includes breathing a turquoise, lapis blue and gold Sacred Geometry Star around you to aid abundance of wisdom and spiritual opportunity

- If you have one, hold one of the Zadkiel crystals in your left hand.
- Close your eyes and start taking deep breaths of Gold energy, breathing out any negative emotions, until you start to feel relaxed.
- Then invoke Zadkiel like this: *Zadkiel, Zadkiel, Zadkiel I ask you to send your Wisdom power of Creation Indigo: the spiralling energy of Jupiter and of your Dominions Angels, to flow into me. Allow me to remember and re-connect to my own wisdom gained in past lives, as I wish to use this for my Highest Good and for the Highest Good of All.*
- Now imagine that you can take deep Wisdom breaths in of Creation Indigo, and that it is interwoven with healing sparkles of lapis, turquoise, and gold.
- Breathe this wonderful, mysterious energy down as spirals, allowing it to permeate throughout your body.
- Become completely filled with Zadkiel's abundance spirals; then ground them in Mother Earth to help her with abundance of healing.
- Then bring them back to your third eye chakra, and feel your perception expand.
- Now breathe out these spirals, saying: *With these rays I breathe your deep blue Sacred Star around me, threaded with turquoise, shining with Gold sparkles, to help me to recognise the abundance of my own ancient wisdom. With heart and soul I shall work with this abundance, in the sacred cause of Love and Light.*

- You may well be able to actually feel/see/sense this star energy around you! What shape Sacred Geometry Star do you have?
- If it's a Six-Point Star* (Macrocosm) then Zadkiel is suggesting that self-healing and Heart Quest is your priority.
- If it's a Five-Point Star* (Microcosm), then Zadkiel says spiritual development and Soul Quest should be your focus.
- If you can't see/sense/feel it, then put your hands above your head – it will be tingly. Don't worry as it's definitely there and should last for about 36-48 hours!
- After this time you would need to repeat the meditation to re-create it.
- If you held a crystal, you will have programmed it with your request, so ask Zadkiel to seal this in and then carry it around to remind you about this exercise*See Sacred Symbols Suit of the Harmony Angel Cards

Some ancient Angelic Wisdom of the Essenes

Wisdom is not always written. Since ancient times there have also been oral wisdom keepers, aided by angels. This extract is from the Apocalypse of Adam, an ancient, probably Essene, testament, found among a cache of Gnostic documents in the Egyptian cliffs at Nag Hammadi in 1945:

"The words they have kept, of the God of the aeons, were not committed to the book, nor were they written. But angelic beings will bring them, whom all the generations of men will not know. For they will be on a high mountain upon a Rock of Truth. Therefore they will be named "The Words of Imperishability and Truth", for those who know the eternal God in wisdom of knowledge and the teaching of angels forever, for He knows All things".

Chapter Eight

Haniel – Venus – Friday

KEY WORDS: LOVE, BEAUTY, JOY, COMPASSION
WITHOUT JUDGEMENT

"A Book of Verses underneath the Bough
A Jug of Wine, a Loaf of Bread – and thou
Beside me singing in the Wilderness – O Wilderness were Paradise
enow (enough)"
From "The Rubaiyat" of Omar Khayyam

The Ancient Wisdom: Haniel, whose name means "Grace of God", rules the third of the Seven Heavens and the planet Venus, the Star of Love, also known as the Morning and/or Evening Star. She is therefore concerned with love, friendship, all relationships and also sexuality. She is chief of the angel order of Virtues in the Angel Hierarchies (angels that beam rose-gold healing around Earth). In the oldest recorded civilisation she was also associated with the Chaldean deity Ishtar, and in ancient Egypt with Hathor. For millennia her name has adorned good luck or love charms. She is also associated with the Malachim Angel Alphabet*, as Malachim is Hebrew for the Virtues Angels. The principal duty of the Order of Virtues Angels is recorded to be that of working healing miracles on Earth, and these angels confer grace and bravery to deserving mankind, depending on the way we treat others. This gives us plenty of scope in which to call upon Haniel for loving support in connection with healing our general, business and loving personal relationships of all kinds. *See Angel Almanac and Love & Light Angel Cards.*

For the 21st Century: Haniel is also concerned with how you relate to your own self-image, and this is in both public and private connections. Are you fully comfortable with yourself and relaxed about how you appear and sound to others? Remember that people will take you at your own face value, therefore if you don't have any sense of self-worth how can you expect others to give you a higher valuation? It can be equally difficult if you appear to be self-confident on the outside, but this is only a façade you are creating, masking an inner lack of security. The longer this goes on, the harder it is to maintain. Hopefully you've already worked on these issues with Camael for courage and Michael for communication. Now seek help from Haniel to assist you to overcome shyness or lack of self-esteem, for she allows you to see your own beauty more clearly and smoothes all relationships. In this chapter you will also see suggestions on finding, and keeping, the right life partner, and Haniel may be called upon any time for good fortune!

Raising spiritual consciousness: Of course there is much more than this to the role Haniel has been given from the Creator, for you will read about mankind's two heart chakras and types of love: Creation Green is Haniel's first colour, and as described above, this is for healing the personal heart, including re-finding and keeping loving relationships in your life. But the angels say that in spiritual terms, this is really to enable you to move through Haniel's pink rose-gold towards Creation Magenta: the colour of the second – higher – heart. This Colour of Creation illuminates a heart that is able to feel unconditional, non-judgemental, love, the love of the angels themselves, and which they hope you will learn to radiate from your own, open heart.

Invoking Haniel in the way you now know
You can invoke Haniel by simply saying *"Haniel, Haniel, Haniel please help me now, in Love and Light, in Love and Light, in Love and*

Light". You, or they (if you are asking for someone else) should receive an immediate feeling of comfort, very often manifested as warmth around your heart, head or hands, or enfolding you like a soft rose pink feathery cloak (see also closing meditation in this chapter). You may also smell roses, one of the flower scents of the angels.

To increase focus with Haniel: especially relevant on Fridays as this is the day of Venus and is ruled by Haniel, you can add:

Candles: any shade of green, and or pink, would be suitable for Haniel.

Her principal crystals are rose quartz, emerald, malachite, jade or tourmaline. These crystals relate to love, friendships and affairs of the heart, while the pink and green in tourmaline signify love yet also growth and abundance. Jade is considered lucky, so that Haniel's name on jade is doubly fortunate. Dioptase and rhodonite are also linked to Haniel.

Essential oils or essences would be rose, rosewood, jasmine, lotus or mandarin, *but remember to take care which you use if pregnant, as some are considered unsuitable for use during pregnancy.*

The metal for Venus is copper. For relationships and love issues and for contentment, copper, as in bracelets or small pieces of this metal, helps to empower any exercises or meditations you do; more about this later in the chapter.

Haniel says: *My Key Words are* **LOVE, BEAUTY, JOY AND COMPASSION,** *all without judgement, and without envy.*

She continues: *To understand what this really means, you need to work with the two heart chakra Colours of Creation: Green and*

Magenta; one heals the personal heart; the other begins to open the higher heart chakra and flower.

Haniel teaches us that as there are two kinds of love, therefore there are two heart chakras within our body. The first is love of a personal nature, such as you feel for a partner, spouse, friend, family and even for yourself; this is primarily drawn through Creation Green – the emerald ray which heals, nourishes and empowers the green chakra of personal heart. Crystals such as emerald and jade will help to balance relationships and heal quarrels, while malachite defuses situations. You must first heal with Creation Green in order to move to the other type of love: the unconditional, non-judgemental love which flows from what is termed your higher heart chakra and resembles the angels' love for us.

As you move forward spiritually in heart you begin to sense pink. This is actually a higher vibration of Creation Red, which comes when you have cleared your root chakra; it begins to flow to heart from the root when root is healed. When you can start to sense rose pink you are letting go of judgement because you feel more secure in life. This is huge spiritual progress: pure compassion for all things on Mother Earth, including self, whatever the faults, as made by the Creator. This unconditional love does not judge and has no limits. It flows from the higher heart chakra of universal love. You could regard these colours within as like a water lily, with Creation Green representing the leaves and bud, and pink, (which with Sacred Nine deepens and becomes Creation Magenta – ninth chakra), for the flower itself. Haniel invites you now to self-heal, to fill yourself with her Colours of Creation rays and to try to appreciate the beauty within all things. Find self-fulfilment through expressing your love, celebrating your existence through appreciation of beauty around you. Choose a medium such as colours, art, music or writing, in fact whatever embodies your creative beauty in a positive way and that when you use it, brings you personal joy. Let it infuse your spirit. Crystals will especially enhance this loving energy, so that it surrounds you with an aura. Love and joy will light you with radiance from within, inspiring others to want it for themselves. Haniel reminds you that in Divine Truth, Love is all you need, and she guides you through this most important spiritual growth. Green of Creation is for calmness: Green heals your emotions as it is linked to the heart chakra, moon and Creation Silver. Both Green and Turquoise (eighth chakra: thymus) link to the Water of Life, ruled by the angel Phuel (see *Harmony Angel Cards*) and balanced by Creation Gold of Sun, ruled by the Angel Raphael.

All of us have been hurt at some time, and unless healed, this can block heart expansion. Creation Green is needed first to allow the heart to open again to love. Deeper shades mean deeper emotions, the paler the shade the more you are healing the situation and moving on. Then pink will begin to flow from the root chakra to the heart, often with Gold of healing. Pink's vibration from Red means more security in love; also contentment and compassion in the heart, as well as enabling you to realise your true self-worth. With enough love you can let go of negative emotions you no longer need, build self-esteem and confidence, and so experience heart empowerment.

Therefore, pink is a first colour of the higher heart and the higher heart flower, meaning you are beginning to see with eye of heart. The flower is often seen as a rose or lily at first, but as you become more spiritual, as mentioned in Camael's chapter it will change colour to Creation Magenta and then change form, if you wish to be a healer, becoming in time the sacred geometry Seed of Life. This is an important healing fractal that can be sent out to All from a heart of unconditional love. In this book we cover Sacred

Seven: the first seven major chakras. But you will already be aware that the next step is Sacred Nine. By bridging the gap between Creation Violet and Red, Magenta closes the rainbow circle of Love and Light and with Creation Turquoise completes the first nine Colours of Creation.

Roses, flowers whose scent calls the angels, are associated with Haniel

- Rose or rosewood oil is especially for heart issues. Rose has a vibration close to the angels (pure positive love energy) and also helps to summon them. Rose opens the heart to love and rosewood works on the crown chakra by aiding you to deepen your Divine connection. When doing meditations with any angel, but particularly with Haniel, you could use a few drops of an essence or oil of either of these to perfume a room, or apply sparingly to pulse points if working with this chapter.

Moving forward, then, if all you need right now is more Love and Joy generally you can start with a daily affirmation with Haniel to gain this in your life.

To affirm your need for Love and Joy:

- *With Haniel I affirm my need for abundant earthly happiness and loving fulfilment. I pledge to find the beauty within me, allowing my own inner radiance to shine out, to attract that someone special I deserve, to whom I can give, and from whom I can receive, love and joy.*

To help yourself, or someone else, such as a friend or loved one, whose heart is emotionally hurt or troubled, you can always invoke Haniel's aid. A suitable invocation would be:

- Haniel, Haniel, Haniel *please bring me your loving support to help my heart (or that of whoever you are asking for) to be healed and to bring joy back into life, in love and light, love and light, love and light.*

- If you want to do this invocation to assist someone else you should always try to get his or her permission first, *remembering that what they are experiencing may be karmic and need to be addressed and overcome by them as a spiritual learning curve.* Failing this, you could still send help, as if rejected it will just come back to you in the form of positive love energy and healing; to give is always to receive.
- Tourmaline also aids healing of the heart, especially if it contains both pink and green heart colours, as does alexandrite (though this is rare and expensive).
- Any small crystal piece can be programmed with one of the meditations in this chapter (see next meditation). After that, you can just give it to a person who needs it, explaining it should be carried until the heart feels soothed.

Working with the two Colours of Creation: first healing with Creation Green:

If you need to heal your personal heart (Green), this helps you to address this, so that you can then move on to work with pink, and begin opening the higher heart of unconditional love. There are two parts to this exercise –The first part links to Green and the second to Green and Pink. So either try this one first or go straight to Part 2:

Part 1: Healing the personal heart and heart-breaks. You can bring in Raphael also for general heart healing (see also his chapter).

- If you wish to programme a green crystal relevant to Haniel at the same time as doing this meditation, hold it in your left, Universal taking hand, while doing the meditation. At the end of the meditation close your right hand over it, asking Haniel to seal in the intention for the Highest Good.

- Next, determine your personal heart healing need: is it physical heart healing, mental hurt or emotional healing that you require, perhaps it's more than one?

- Breathe in deep, golden, Raphael healing breaths, breathing out negative, dark, emotions, until you feel filled with angelic Love and Light and ready to continue.

- Remember Creation Green helps heal your personal heart of sadness or grief and emotional or mental hurt caused by loss or rejection. Or if you have had a physical heart illness, it can soothe, strengthen, and help you regain confidence once more.

- Focus within on your heart – the energy centre that is your heart space.

- In your heart space visualise a green bubble holding Water of Life, and floating on the water is a green water lily leaf – this all represents the personal heart chakra

- Next say the words *"Haniel, Haniel, Haniel I ask for your Creation Green ray to flow in to heal my heart of past hurts."*

- Really try to feel this ray of sparkling, translucent emerald flowing into your heart space; see it energise the bright Water of Life bubble, visualize this soothing emotion, and ask Haniel to help your healing process begin.

- Will and intend any dark areas that are your past hurts, and that you are willing now to release, to flow into the Water of Life to be healed, (they will be rendered harmless and released down to Earth) until the Water of Life glows and sparkles.

- Keep doing this until you feel your heart become lighter

and the Green more vivid; (you may see a water lily bud appear on the leaf).

- Then WILL this sparkling Green Love and Light healing out to All, or down to Mother Earth; in return more healing will flow back to your heart.
- When you sense you have attained a level of healing that feels beneficial and calming, and you see the bubble as clear, and the leaf as bright, ask Haniel to seal in this healing and thank all the angels you invoked.

Copper: the metal of Venus and Love, and adding Michael's mirrors, for thoughtfulness in love

- If you are embarking on a new relationship and want to say and do the right things, wear something to remind you of Haniel, who tells us that *Copper contains power of love and that we should wear or carry a piece of copper to guide our loving thoughts and words and to bring her energy into our everyday life.*

- Place your pink or green crystal or piece of copper on a mirror (for Michael). This magnifies the energy of your crystal and metal manifold. If you are looking for a partner, ask Haniel from your heart saying *Haniel, Haniel, Haniel, please help me to re-open my heart and to find my true life partner, for my Highest Good.* You might even catch a glimpse in the mirror of the person with whom you will next fall in love, for with the mirror you are adding mercury, therefore Michael's energy, so also seeking your truth!

Perhaps to attract more love, such as a new relationship, you need to change your perspective on life? Haniel counsels:
My message is purely and simply one of Love and Light, for really that

is all you need. Light eternally threads the Universe with rainbow filaments; Love is the power that binds and heals All. When you grasp this Truth and send Love out from your own higher heart, though you may not "see" it you are actually giving physical form to Light with a view to aiding others.

My task is to first bring rays of Creation Green and later, when you are ready, rose-gold to heal and pink to unfold your heart flower, for I teach you the power of love in all its many aspects. My rays of Angelic Light begin, respectively, the process of healing and then opening your higher heart, allowing you to recognise the beauty in all creation, so that your heart flowers with true unselfish love and compassion. Do not worry if the contemplation of beauty moves you to tears – this is Spirit – simply the sublime breath of angels communing directly with your heart and becoming Water of Life for you to release emotional blocks.

And I am here to offer you the Light in my rose pink mirror* of Love in order for you to see yourself more clearly. You do not need to have an actual mirror. All you need to do is to imagine my special golden mirror facing you, and know that it is filled with Love and rose-coloured Light. If you look in this mirror and practise using the eye of heart as well as your normal eyes, you will learn to be able to see your true self – a beautiful being: a being of Grace who is a reflection of All. When you can love yourself unconditionally then you can start to love others, faults and all, for you have let go of judgement and found true compassion.

Let yourself surrender to love and beauty, and allow me to fill your heart with my own healing Colours of Creation. You will then see that these will overflow into your surroundings, helping those around you to also be healed and fulfilled, for love can transcend and heal all situations. Also, the power of love emanates positive vibrations from the heart and these attract new people into your life.

This is your chance to allow Light to prevail and Love to flower in and around your life; then nothing is impossible, for this is the key to All.

103

The pink mirror is pictured in both A Harmony of Angels and An Angel for Every Day, and also referred to in the Angel Almanac.

Compassion for self is hard for most of us

Haniel's remit is all types of beauty and she helps you to especially recognise beauty of self. If you find it hard to appreciate the beauty in yourself (and most of us do find this hard), or forgive yourself for something in the past, try this meditation with Haniel, using her pink mirror of Love.

This exercise with Haniel can actually help you to "see" your own beautiful self and you can use it to download the Attunement. You can also invite in Camael for courage, Michael for strength, Zadkiel for abundance of angelic help, and any other member of the Sacred Seven whose help you need.

- Sit down and close your eyes, ensuring you are comfortable for 15 or 20 minutes.
- Imagine you are sitting facing Haniel's round, pink, Mirror of Love; it is as large as you and so it reflects your whole self.
- First call Haniel by saying *Haniel, Haniel, Haniel please be with me as I breathe in the power of your roses and Love. I ask for your connective Angelic Light Attunement to aid me. As I breathe out, help me to let go of feelings of unworthiness so that I can begin to achieve my true potential and to live life for my highest good.*
- Now start breathing as deeply as possible, imagining with each breath you are drawing in rose pink energy from Above, through self, right down to the base of your spine.
- On the out-breaths, try to let go of worry so that the angels can disperse it.
- When you feel filled with a column of pink energy, imagine you can send this from root chakra to Below; to Mother

Earth herself, who sustains you.

- Imagine you are held between Above and Below in a column of Love, lit by pure, shining pink Light.
- Now, focus within, in your heart, and you can view with the eye of the heart.
- Visualise Haniel's large, round, pink mirror directly in front of you, facing you.
- Ask Haniel to reflect back to you, from her mirror of Love, awareness of how to let go of hurt and to see and recognise your own beauty, saying that you wish to become your true self for your Highest Good.
- Mentally note whatever you glimpse, sense, feel or hear intuitively in the next few seconds; this is your guide from Haniel about your healing priority and how to move on physically and spiritually in this life.
- Graciously accept Haniel's guidance. (*Don't try to rationalise what you seemed to be shown or told, as you are then involving the head instead of the heart*).
- If everything is not entirely resolved the first time KEEP DOING this exercise, "glimpsing" more that you need to address and release, until you can feel things changing for you. You may have to eradicate a mind-set you have had for many years. If this is the case, return to the Michael chapter and do this with Michael's Light Sword.
- Really try to see yourself more positively and as more fortunate than others, rather than less fortunate, and always thank Haniel for her loving assistance.

Other ways Haniel assists us

- As mentioned, Haniel is also an angel of good luck and good fortune; call on Haniel for this if you feel you need it.
- Also, Haniel is especially protective of babies and children, to protect little folk call on her for this and ask for

her help with this.

If you *even now* feel your heart is still closed, or frozen, perhaps your hurt is embedded deeper still. You may need to bring it out, go back and work with Camael again to forgive the person(s) who caused it, so that you can open to true compassion.

Or do you need to forgive yourself for something you did? Note: Phanuel is the Guardian Angel of Atonement and you can invoke him if necessary.

Either way, Haniel helps you to do this with pale rose-gold energy in the following forgiveness meditation by allowing you to open more fully to love and compassion. You can also invite Rachmiel, who incarnated as St. Francis of Assisi, and/or Terathel** both of whom are tasked by the Creator with helping us to open to compassion and the power of unconditional love for All. **Rachmiel can be found in the Harmony Angel Cards and Terathel in the Love & Light Angel Cards*

- Close your eyes and breathe deeply of the rose-gold healing breath of Haniel's Virtues Group of healing angels, releasing any dark, negative emotions, until you start to feel relaxed and filled with Light, especially in the Green heart chakra.
- Focus on this chakra, and try to visualise a green flower bud within it (e.g. a rose).
- If you need to forgive someone who hurt you, instead of bitterness or hatred you felt up until now, *try to feel compassion* for this person, and to mentally picture him or her *within* the rose bud, *it may even be that you need to picture yourself there.*
- Then invoke Haniel like this: *Haniel, Haniel, Haniel, I ask you for the power and warmth of your loving compassion. Let this*

flow into me, comforting me, let me now feel this compassion, for myself and for all others, for my ultimate Highest Good, in Love and Light, Love and Light, Love and Light.

- Now breathe in more rose-gold energy; with each breath you are breathing it deeper into yourself, into your heart *willing it* to become bathed in Light.
- As rose-gold energy pours into the rose bud it also, if you willed and intended it to do so, reaches the person(s) you have placed there, because rose-gold is a healing vibration of unconditional Love.
- *If you can do this with total honesty of intention*, the rose will begin to unfold and it will be bright pink* in colour, edged with gold; the energy will then grow brighter and radiate from the rose of your heart into your whole self: mind, body and spirit, infusing all with the warmth of that compassion. (*You may see various shades, possibly Creation Magenta if releasing a past life block)*
- Now, as you continue to breathe this rose gold energy in and out it gradually forms rosy Wings of Light around you.
  - You may actually be able to feel this tingling energy around you.
  - The Light Wings announce you have moved on from Creation Green towards the higher heart opening and that you are radiating Love &Light.
  - As you bring your focus back to the heart and then the mind, remember to thank Haniel for her help.
  - You can repeat this as often as you need, to free your heart as well as to renew the rose-gold Light Wings, with Haniel's loving assistance.

If you did the previous exercise you will have moved along the way in freeing yourself from the past and now you have begun to channel rose-gold compassion try part two of the exercise for spiritual harmony.

Part 2: Steps to open the higher heart.

In this version you invoke Haniel, again you may want to invite Rachmiel and Terathel. Both are specific angels for compassion, bringing shades of rose pink and spiritual Magenta and White Fire, as well as Creation Gold. However, we first repeat the work with Creation Green because there are always new personal heart levels we can heal, once we know how, in order to continue to raise our vibration closer to that of the angels. We also return to the visualisation of the water lily leaf and bud for the higher heart flower; remember this represents unconditional love for all life and especially for self, important if you tend to be self-critical or push yourself to strive for too much perfection.

- If you wish to programme a crystal this time, choose a pink one, a green one or one that is both pink and green. Follow the procedure as for part one.
- To open the higher heart you will need to let go of judgement of self and others and to feel compassion for Mother Earth and All Life.
- Begin by breathing in deep, golden, healing breaths, breathing out any more negative, dark, emotions, until you feel filled with angelic Love, and plenty of Raphael's healing Creation Gold Light to help empower new decisions.
- If necessary, ask for this Light to show you if there are other aspects of self you need to address to be able to open your heart flower. Bear in mind you may need to go back to other chapters to work on those aspects.
- Next focus on your own heart and its two combined healing symbols. Visualise a bubble containing a green pool. Floating on this is a green lily leaf for the personal heart chakra and a green bud containing a pink water lily.

NB: The pink lily or lotus is a traditional symbol of the open higher heart chakra.

- Now say the words "Haniel, Haniel, Haniel let Creation Green flow in".
- See Creation Green flow into the pool and how crystal clear it now is; accessing more Green can simply take you to a new level of vibration of personal heart.
- Then say "Haniel, Haniel, Haniel, I am ready to open higher heart, I realise that in healing, to give is to receive manifold; please allow me your pink-rose-gold rays to open up the heart flower petal by petal.
- Really put Love into this to make it happen and witness the water lily unfolding.
- Now ask Raphael, Rachmiel and Terathel for their Angelic Light Rays to flow in, filling the flower with more of this pure energy.
- When all pink petals (usually six) are infused with White and edged with Gold, unconditional love and compassion has been ignited within your heart. Then, with all your heart WILL this love, healing and compassion out into all corners of Mother Earth, in return manifold healing will flow back into your heart, gradually opening it further.
- This is a huge spiritual step because even though you may as yet still need to move fully from Seven to Nine in terms of Creation Colours and chakras, *your higher heart of unconditional Love is the bridge between lower and higher self.*
- Repeating this exercise as often as you can allows you to move your healing focus from the heart bridge towards your higher self (throat, third eye and crown) and thus allows you to attain a new level of spiritual development (Dance of Five).
- Always send Love and Light and thanks to all the angels you invoked.

Finally, a visualisation to re-affirm Haniel's comforting presence;

this is with rose quartz to fill your healed and opened heart with greater Love, Light and Joy in life

- Take some deep breaths of the White Fire ray also called Spiritus Dei, that is the Breath of God. As you do this, expel negative thoughts from your mind, until you feel filled with loving energy.
- Ground this energy through your feet, sending love down to Mother Earth and bringing it back through your body, to your crown.
- Invoke Haniel and other angels you have chosen to be with you.
- They offer you an etheric crystal of rose quartz and invite your spirit to go within its heart – you are completely enveloped in the rose pink Light of Joy that heals sadness, you can feel the comforting energy of rose quartz fill you.
- Even if you can't "see" it, just "know" you are there!
- Feel the presence of the angels of Love all around you, and perhaps you can smell the scent of the roses, a perfume close to the angelic vibration.
- The angels' wings softly enfold you – feel them like a million soft feathers intermingled with fragrant rosy petals.
- Ask the angels to help you find and keep Love in your life, so that you may give it also to others, for Love binds the Universe together.
- See rose quartz Light Rays encircling your heart and flowing into the bright flower you now hold within, which you see glowing with Love.
- Ask the angels to seal this energy in for you, so you can keep that sense of heart healing and renewal.
- You can also do this for loved ones and visualise their hearts similarly energised.
- Send Love, Light and thanks to the angels.

More Ancient Angelic Wisdom of the Essenes

Around the time of Jesus the Essenes had established themselves as a strict and deeply religious sect of Jews who believed that daily communion with angels enabled the harmonisation of physical and spiritual self. These practices were termed *angelology* and were considered essential for wholeness. Since the discovery of the Dead Sea Scrolls, which were believed to have been written by the Essenes and hidden before their massacre by the Romans in 70 AD, it is generally believed that Jesus himself was an Essene initiate, though the scrolls do not specifically name him; only referring to the Teacher of Righteousness. The following extract from the Essene Mysteries (translated from the Hebrew by T.H. Gaster) is a Poem of Initiation probably written by the Teacher of Righteousness, and indicates the strength of Essene angelic beliefs:

Angels of wondrous strength
Minister unto thee
And they walk at the side of the meek
And of them that are fearful of right doing
And of all the lost and (for)lorn
Who stand in need of mercy
Lifting them out of the slough
When that their feet are mired.

Chapter Nine

Cassiel – Saturn – Saturday

KEY WORDS: OVERCOMING CHALLENGE, PEACE, HARMONY, SERENITY

"Waste not this precious hour to live in Yesterday
It is not "This" or "That" but "How" we live and pray,
Forget the bitter fruit be jocund with the Grape,
'Twill turn to Wine and you can see a blessed Angel Shape."
From "Lumifar" – J.C. Rutledge

The Ancient Wisdom: Cassiel ("Speed of God") is the Angel of Solitude and Tears, Ruler of the Order of Cherubim, and the Planet Saturn, Gatekeeper of the Seventh Heaven (as it is written that this is the abode of, and so ruled by, the Creator). One legend describes Cassiel as being swiftest of wing. The Bible describes Cherubim as having four wings as well as four heads, though I have never seen or sensed them like that and I was born on a Saturday! Cassiel is also traditionally called the Angel of Temperance.

For the 21st Century: Temperance is not a word commonly used today. It means seeking to live as moderate and harmonious a life as possible. Is your life tranquil, balanced and unified, or are you overcome by stress or, like most of us, distracted by something challenging that you need to overcome? The latter could include coming to terms with sorrow or loss of some kind: a dark period in life. So often we are caught up in so many day-to-day dramas that we end up "fire-fighting". That is to say, we are dealing with the effects of our problems and not the causes. Cassiel's Planet of Saturn throws us all kinds of challenges to overcome, many of which are karmic, so that we can grow through these experiences towards Light. The point is how we address such challenges. Do you make time for yourself to calmly consider how to rise above them and so to return to peace and serenity? It is up to us to allow some space for contemplation – to identify the cause of our disharmony and try to deal with it at source. Two other important points to remember when eliminating causes of strife are: from a position of knowledge can come inspired action, and challenge can be converted into opportunity. Furthermore, only from experience do we gain wisdom.

Raising spiritual consciousness: As you now know, some two thousand years ago, the Essenes believed that to eliminate disharmony it was necessary to harmonise the spiritual with the physical, thus achieving wholeness, and that a key to this was communing with angels on a daily basis. What greater desire can we have today than to try to achieve such harmony, not only within but also with nature and our surroundings? If you are dealing with bereavement, sorrow or rejection you may feel at times that you are alone and surrounded by darkness. In fact, the Divine White Fire spark is within all of us, even though we may have forgotten about it, causing it to be dormant within the heart. If we *will and intend it,* we can once again ignite that spark and become part of the Oneness, or, we may even attain Unity Consciousness. We (Microcosm) mirror Nature's sacred geometric perfection of form, expressed in Five through the Golden Mean, Phi ratio and DNA. This, in turn is but a galactic fragment of the Universe, itself – Macrocosm: All That Is, expressed first by Six*. By understanding this, by respecting Mother Earth and all sentient life, and by striving to re-harmonise within and without, we can regain equilibrium.
*Dance of Six and Five

Cassiel will invite you now to begin to let go of the past, without in any way diminishing its importance to your development, which will allow you to once again achieve his qualities of peace, harmony and serenity.

Try invoking Cassiel to see how you respond to his special energy:

- *Cassiel, Cassiel, Cassiel, please help me rediscover harmony (or peace or serenity), in life, in Love and Light, Love and Light, Love and Light.*

Cassiel says: *my Key Words are:* **OVERCOMING CHALLENGE TO REGAIN PEACE, HARMONY, SERENITY;** *all attributes which contribute towards your understanding of the true meaning of Oneness with All.*

To increase focus with Cassiel on any day, but especially on the day he rules which is Saturday:

Choose a pure white candle for Cassiel.

His crystals are obsidian (including snowflake – Apache Tears – and gold sheen), onyx, rutilated quartz and black or black and white agate. Onyx protects against enemies. Black agate is for courage. Smoky quartz helps with raising energy and clearing depression. Onyx holds power. Black and white crystals invite balance.

Cassiel's metal is lead, and is usually easier to buy when combined with tin to make pewter. A small piece of pewter, or a bowl, would add more focus and can also be used when working with Zadkiel, whose metal is tin.

Life's ups and downs

Cassiel shows us the rays of light and shade, for in this reality, for all of us, there *is* always going to be duality – happiness and sadness, laughter and tears, positive and negative, darkness and Light. The karmic lessons are given to us because without one, the other cannot be fully appreciated, and Cassiel reminds us that by perseverance and by converting challenge to opportunity it *is* possible to move forward from dark situations and back into Light. You need to reflect on what lesson you are being asked to learn, what karma you are re-dressing. Remember that Camael told you bitterness constricts the soul, so that forgiveness is needed, while Haniel taught that love and compassion brings about soul's expansion to serenity. It may be that you are in the midst of pain or sorrow right now. Cassiel gives comfort in the dark night of the soul, allowing you to once more perceive Light and work with him towards it.

Seeking harmony and balance in life means taking the time to think about inner peace, to be at one (and a-tone) with oneself. It also means being in tune with nature and the environment. Instead of feeling separate from everything, begin to seek Oneness (with Mother Earth and All Life) or Unity Consciousness (Oneness with the Universe or even the Omniverse). Cassiel says that the first step is to be able to deal with challenge, rather than resenting it, and to be able to overcome it in the way the angels suggest. By this I mean by choosing to send love and compassion to everyone and every-thing on Mother Earth. The more you send out, the more you will receive in return, with the bonus that you will gradually move towards peace and harmony with all life and once more become part of what you could call the sacred geometry that comprises the Cosmic Web.

Comparing Unity Consciousness and Oneness with All

These are linked states which have different levels of meaning. Oneness firstly means being joined through the higher heart to everything in Earth (Below) and Sky (Above), feeling love and compassion for any and all sentient life – from mankind to trees, plants, animals, birds and insects – even earth, rock, crystal and mountain. Unity Consciousness takes a wider view, and to me, implies channelling and working from the higher heart with unfallen, pure Light. This goes far beyond this world and its reality, into the Universe, Multiverse, even Omniverse. It means respecting All, helping to heal All, working for the benefit of All.

Overcoming challenge in life by addressing issues that may have prevented your inner peace and harmony

A comforting Cassiel channelling about life's challenges

This will help you face and overcome personal challenges you've had that could be blocking your energy, or perhaps you are even now facing in life.

I pierce that which you call night with my glorious White rays, pinpointing the eternal contrast of darkness and Light. All will encounter this contrast in life's journey, but I lead the way back through Love to the pure Light that flows from those who feel peace and serenity. I hold the Gate of the Seventh Heaven that can only be passed by those souls who accept that there will be opposite forces of energy in life, and that there is both a need and a lesson in reconciling them. It is I who comes to help you to balance the life you are living now, your happiness and sadness, high points and occasionally, despair: your own Light and shade situations. I come to comfort you at those latter times, when life has seemed to be against you, for my role is to help you through and bring you slowly back to peace and harmony, with the knowledge that when the hour seems darkest, Light is nonetheless never far away, and indeed you will have made spiritual progress with the widom you gained from this experience.

Consider a bracelet made of individual links, shaded one link at a time from black towards white. If you start at the black link, each next link grows paler, when you get to the pure white link then the very next one is black! The contrast serves to emphasise the difference, and so it is with life. All lives contain some suffering, and this makes the happiness an even more precious gift to enjoy. To suffer is to learn understanding, sympathy and compassion – though often coupled with a desire to be alone. However, to be filled with joy is to want to share a little of this with others, touching lives like a sudden sunbeam on a wintry day.

If you have suffered, or are suffering, grief or loss, you need not do so in solitude. In the dark and lonely night of the soul, when tears overwhelm; mine is the loving comfort you can invoke to be with you. I enfold you within my gentle, consoling Light Wings to comfort you, as I gradually heal and strengthen you. You will perceive the White Fire of my Angelic Light blaze your trail towards a more promising new dawn.

Cassiel assists you to re-find serenity after a particularly dark or difficult situation:

- Cassiel reminds you that if you have just gone through a difficult or dark period in your life *it may have been caused by karmic issues you agreed to face and overcome in this lifetime.* By accepting this situation, finding some redeeming aspect to the negative offered, and working through your challenge to achieve a positive outcome, you will be freed to move on. Strive to see what the angels are trying to teach you, so you don't have to go through such a situation again.
- To understand Cassiel's message better place a piece of obsidian, and a piece of selenite side by side on your desk or table, or you could use snowflake obsidian or black and white agate. It is said that the darkest time of the night is just before dawn. If you are having a hard time, *just look at*

these crystals and consider that, as day follows night, this, too will pass; then ask Cassiel for the strength and wisdom to see it through!

Anafiel, Guardian Angel of Heavenly Peace, adds her advice as it is relevant to this chapter:

Heavenly peace resides in the higher heart, the heart of your personal heart. You can reach it if you try, on The Way of Love and Light, but first you must let go of, and heal the past. I hope you began this with Camael. To help you to go further, put up my name with Cassiel's, Camael's and Haniel's. Whenever you have a quiet moment, invoke the four of us to support you towards healing and opening the higher heart. You will be aided by the next special exercise with Cassiel, for once you know the Way, you can always return there in times of need – and there will be those times.

Yet as I, Cassiel and Haniel tell you:

If you have opened the higher heart flower, then there are always advanced stages to attain as you grow spiritually, for as Zadkiel has vouchsafed, it is all linked to ancient wisdom, and wisdom has neither beginning nor end, for in its end is always a new beginning. He has also told you that As Above So Below and this, in your 21st Century, is what I wish you to comprehend. As you might say "in terms of spirituality there is All to play for".

When you have succeeded in opening the higher heart, the most important new wisdom beginning is when the higher heart flower awakens further to become crystalline*. That step begins with the Seed of Life, a sacred geometry that, if you have enough Love, expands into the Flower of Life. It is a fractal that you can learn how to send out to help heal All. A fractal can be any size, infinitely large or small, but never diminishes in its power, and this particular sacred geometry is the first true and complete healing pattern; consequently it is extremely *important, not just for mankind, but for Mother Earth herself and the Nature Kingdom. You can therefore see that every step you take in heart and soul to open to us, the angels, and to work with us daily to learn these secrets, is taking you nearer to As Below, So Above and to creating Heavenly Peace on Earth.* *Awakening the Crystalline Heart*

Finding or re-finding peace, harmony and serenity with Cassiel

This exercise is with Cassiel and your Primary Guardian Angel of the day of the week you were born on. You can use it to download your Cassiel Attunement.

- Invoke the angel Cassiel to be with you. Begin to take deep breaths, imagining that you are breathing in his White Light, and breathing out more dark energy: sad, angry or bitter things you are now ready to release from yourself.
- Keep releasing more negative issues. As you continue breathing deeply in and out you are gradually filling your energy meridian to overflowing with White Light.
- Then, as you breathe out, White Light begins to swirl around you, gently expanding outwards in a spiral, until there is enough to form a circular tunnel of White stretching away from you.
- When ready, and with Michael protecting your physical body, let your consciousness travel along the tunnel; see a sphere of Michael's Creation Blue at the end of it.
- Count down from ten as you start to go along the tunnel, reaching one as you come to the end, and so you prepare to step outside.
- You emerge from the tunnel into a beautiful place in nature. You are in a grassy meadow, beside a clear stream that gently flows over rocks and boulders, making a soft splashing sound. There are brightly coloured birds and butterflies that show no fear of you; the sun is shining

warmly. The meadow is full of fragrant wild flowers and herbs. *Try to note their colour(s).*

- Now *view with the eye of heart*: you find that you can see the energy that makes up everything around you. You, and they, are translucent, formed of sparkling rainbow Light. Instead of appearing solid every single item is made of millions of Light energy particles dancing in the sunshine.

- Filaments of Light appear, connecting you in geometric patterns to everything you can see, and connecting every single thing to you. See that you are in Oneness – part of the collective consciousness. The rainbow Light of the Cosmic Web is formed of geometry; it stretches like gossamer, fine but strong for it is Love that binds All together.

- Ask Casssiel for your connective Angelic Light Attunement.

- Now Cassiel takes your hand (*one or more Guardian Angels may take your other hand*). You fly upwards, from Below into sky and Above.

- You become aware that geometric filaments of light join you also to Raphael's Sun, Gabriel's Moon and even the Stars. You are truly part of the Macrocosmic Universe and you marvel at the revelation.

- You see that you can send Love and Light to the Universe from your heart. Then, magnified, it radiates back along the filaments, filling you too with Love and Light, completing the Circle of spiritual renewal.

- Cassiel and your Guardian Angel return you gently to your pure White Light tunnel, reminding you that you can draw in the Light to yourself and expel darkness by carrying out this exercise at any time.

- Breathe gently to bring back your focus to now and open your eyes when ready.

- Thank Cassiel and your Guardian Angel for their loving care and remember that you can return to this meadow whenever you wish.

- If you work hard with the angels in this book and continue to do so, you will find that your heart begins to reach a permanent state of Oneness, so that in effect, you've brought Heaven and Heavenly Peace to Earth as Anafiel suggested.

This visualisation offers many opportunities. Firstly it is a chance to be aware of one or more of your Guardian Angels at this time. Ensure that you immediately note down the angels who appeared. Do this as soon as you open your eyes. Also, the colour or colours of the flowers you saw will pinpoint your chakra healing priorities. Red will be the root chakra, orange, sacral chakra and so on. Note these before you move on to healing with Raphael in the next chapter. (*NB: I also address this in a systematic way in my book The Angel Quest of the Heart that tells my own story of Rainbow Angel Healing*)

Cassiel: Gatekeeper of Seventh Heaven

If you work with Cassiel he is also the Gatekeeper of the Seventh Heaven, and he will support your quest for Oneness. As you progress, remember to focus outwards; look out for signs in Nature from Cassiel and other angels as these will guide you forward.

Cassiel reminds you: *Sometimes if you suddenly notice an animal: a horse, cat or dog, of black and white, it is a sign I am near you. As you know, black and white signify the two extremes, highest to lowest, darkest to lightest, without and within. As you traverse the Way I am the power that helps you navigate the two extremes, showing you the route between that ultimately brings you back to harmony and balance, for I guide you in the vital knowledge of one to enable the recognition and understanding of the other.*

Zuphlas, Guardian Angel of Trees, adds:
It is I who dapples the light and shade that flows around you when you look at the sky from under one of my magnificent forest trees. Both are necessary for Nature herself, as well as for you, and like the seasons of your year, together they are harmony.

Cassiel Meditation for serenity

If this especially resonates with you, and you find yourself becoming more aware of black and white, light and shade, and how to balance the two, try this meditation with Cassiel, Camael, Raphael and Gabriel. Use intuition to see how to emerge with serenity from past situations and move forward again into Light.

- Sit quietly and close your eyes; place the challenge(s) you face in your heart.
- If you have a Cassiel crystal, hold this in your left hand.
- Invoke Cassiel by saying: Cassiel, Cassiel, Cassiel please be with me to help me face and conquer this challenge for my Highest Good.
- Breathe as deeply as possible, imagining you are breathing pure White (Spiritus Dei) energy in, right down through your body, even into your toes.
- With each out-breath you are letting go of negative feelings, such as fear or worry about what you are facing, until you have let it all go.
- With the next breath send this White energy through your toes and down to the heart of Mother Earth, until it connects with the crystal at her heart.
- Now draw this crystal energy back through your toes, up to your root chakra, asking Camael to once again re-affirm your roots and foundations now that you have worked much more on self-healing, so that you can grow more easily and strongly towards Light.
- Bring the sparkling crystalline energy up into the heart,

with Haniel's help, and then ask Gabriel to help you *intuit* how to overcome your challenge. Ask Camael for any necessary courage, and Raphael to aid you in making your decisions.

- Now bring this energy up to the throat and third eye, asking Michael to illuminate your mind with truth, and Zadkiel for the wisdom to clarify your decision so the outcome will return you to peace and serenity.

- Finally ask Cassiel to help you seal in your positive feelings, and also to complete the programming of your crystal, as you cover this with right hand. Thank him for his help and thank the other angels you invoked.

- Keep the crystal with you for confidence until your challenge is resolved!

- If you are not sure at first, keep doing this exercise until you see the Way forward.

Understanding Angelic Numerology: If, right now, you are currently facing a major challenge in life, become aware that the angels may be trying to give you guidance!

- **Number 1**: The number of energy itself, so that 11 and 111 multiply this energy and link to the root chakra and Creation Red. Start with 1 and Red if you wish to ascend to 9 on the angels' Light ladder of healing.

- **Number 2**: This is the number of a potential new phase in life, while seeing 22 signifies that this change is important – transformational – for you. 222 is the spiritual aspect of transformation. Linked to the sacral chakra, Fire and Creation Orange, it is about innovation and creativity, so prepare to make those decisions!

- **Number 3**: This number firstly indicates a pending

decision about that potential new phase in life, while 33 means the decision/phase is important and 333 signifies spiritual growth. Three also links to the solar chakra and Creation Yellow and Gold of Sun. See also The Law of Three of Hermes Trismegistus.

- **Number 4**: The number of the 4th (personal heart) chakra, linking to love and Creation Green, while with 44 and 444 the angels urge opening of the higher heart of unconditional love and compassion: Creation Magenta.

- **Number 5**: This is an extremely important number because it relates to raising spiritual consciousness. It is linked to the Dance of Five, the Five-point Star of Microcosm and Creation Blue of Truth (throat chakra). If you see 55 this means you can reach the next, higher level of your spiritual development, at 555 you are attaining mastery of this new level.

- **Number 6**: This is a number of healing and completion, as symbolised in the six-pointed star of Macrocosm (All That Is – also known as the Star of David). 66 and higher multiples are not bad (this idea is a mistranslation of the Bible). Multiples of six mean a new level of healing has been reached on your Dance of Six, preparing you for attaining a new vibration in your Dance of Five.

- **Number 7**: As you know this is an extremely important esoteric number figuring in almost all belief systems. It symbolises Mystery, Magic and Alchemy. Also it is the number of Melchisadec, Ruler of the Rainbow, the Sacred Seven and the seventh Violet Ray who holds the invisible, seventh central point of balance in the six-pointed star (Macrocosm).

- **Number 8**: If you see 8 this is for Eternity and connects to the Zodiac Angels whose spiritual "Mother" is Pistis Sophia. Therefore she is both Heavenly and Earthly Mother and the personification of faith, wisdom and compassion. 88 and 888 guide you towards understanding that Light is eternal and retrieving Astrology and Star wisdom.

- **Numbers 9 and 10**: If you see 9, or 99, this indicates that what you started in 3, or 33, 333, is now nearing completion; time to look for fresh guidance from the angels. (This is also the number linked to the re-Ascension of Earth and mankind, a programme which began with the various "Falls" from Grace).

- **Number 11** repeats the message of 1, but you will have "ascended" to 9 have "descended" from 9 back down to 1 in order to be able to "re-ascend" at a higher vibration than before; this is a Phoenix moment!

- **Numbers 12 and 13** are higher vibrations, and indicate reaching the Higher Dance of Twelve and Thirteen. As are quadruple numbers; these are all for another book.

Ancient Angelic Wisdom – Zoroastrianism

Probably the oldest written source of angels is from the Zoroastrian Magi of Chaldea (the land of Abraham and from whose later ranks we see the Three Wise Men of the Bible). They believed in seven levels of the Universe. At its highest levels were Archangels, Gods, and Planetary Deities. Then came Angels, below whom were human souls, while on the level below these came Elementals and the Devic Kingdom. Demons were on the level below that one. The first Zoroaster, father of this philosophy – there may have been five or six who held the title – was believed by Plutarch to have lived over seven thousand years ago. Interestingly, legends say that Zoroaster will have thirteen lives and each time he will be magically reborn through water. (Thirteen – Twelve Around One – is also linked to Ascension & Beyond). The following extract from The Apocalypse of Adam, found in 1945 in the Nag Hammadi Library, probably refers to Zoroaster; it describes Thirteen Incarnations and beautifully illustrates early references to Water of Life.

"She came down to the world below in order to gather flowers, she became pregnant with the desire of the flowers; she gave birth to him in that place. The angels of the flower garden nurtured him. He received glory there and power. And thus he came on the water.

More about haloes of pure Light

Haloes of Light (probably White Fire) are traditionally visible in certain circumstances. The word "chakra" is Sanskrit for "wheel" and because the energy of each chakra is three dimensional, when we reach the crown, the energy (Angelic Light) forms a kind of sphere or helmet of pure White Fire (the Fire That Does Not Burn and the sum of the Colours of Creation) around the head. Once it was thought that only Light Beings such as angels and Saints could have haloes. However, if we are prepared to personally strive to attain Oneness, move then towards Unity Consciousness, and also dedicate ourselves to working in service to the cause of Love and Light, we, too, may just possibly be able to radiate White Fire for others. We may not detect it ourselves (and we should not try as this would be playing to lesser ego!) Others may see or sense it, but it is always vital to remember that the key to service, and travelling the Way of Love & Light, is to retain your humility and your principles, despite the many and various temptations that life throws at us.

When your spirit accesses White Fire I call this The Cloud of Knowing, as if and when you are able to enter this Cloud it brings "inner knowing" of your soul purpose in this life path, and perhaps even beyond.

Chapter Ten

Raphael – Sun – Sunday

KEY WORDS: ENERGY HEALING & KNOWLEDGE, ATTAINING MASCULINE (GOLD) BALANCE FOR DECISIONS & ACTIONS,

"I am the Angel of the Sun, whose flaming wheels begin to run, when God's almighty breath said to the darkness and the Night, let there be Light! And there was Light"
From "Golden Legend" – Longfellow

The Ancient Wisdom: Of ancient origin (Ancient Egypt as Ra), Raphael ("God has healed") has, since ancient times, been charged with the healing of the earth. Sacred texts recorded that through him the earth is made a suitable dwelling place for man, whom he also assists with healing of all maladies. He is Ruler of the Sun, the Second Heaven and the West Wind that can bring about change although healing is undoubtedly his main responsibility. Legends about him also state he assisted Solomon with the building of the famous Temple by bringing him a ring that was able to subdue spirits, so that they built the Temple for him. His crystals are those that reflect all colours – clear quartz or diamond (if you are lucky enough), plus citrine, topaz and sunstone; these give energy at all levels and develop hidden talents.

For the 21st Century: We are all made up of energy and are born with the capacity to either embrace the world and be positive, or turn our back on it, allowing negativity to dominate. If we are ill, doctors can prescribe drugs to alleviate the symptoms, but our problems may be more deeply rooted and even derive from past life experiences. In breathing and eating we absorb energy in and out of our physical body all the time; an exchange that only stops with death! However, what we are taking in, or how we are doing this is equally important. Many people breathe too shallowly, depriving themselves of sufficient energy; others have a poor diet lacking vitamins and minerals. This depletes the body chakras and therefore health. The Zoroastrian philosophy, existing long before Christianity, proclaimed the importance of Earth as our Mother, plus Breath of Life, Fire of Life and Water of Life for health and wellbeing. If negative thought patterns are constantly absorbed and retained, they will damage all subtle energy bodies: physical, emotional, mental, spiritual and etheric, leading to illness. Negativity can come from outside or can be within oneself, engendered by strong emotions such as guilt, resentment, anger, fear or hatred; these can be behavioural patterns that take a great deal of effort and strength of will to modify. The good news is *angels can help and support us to release this negativity.* As Patron of Healers and Healing, Raphael is the most important angel who can be invoked in this connection. Raphael is also especially supportive of all healers.

Raising spiritual consciousness: Energy healing is the gift of Spirit, and if we did but know it, we are surrounded by this: it is conveyed via Love and Light – the most powerful forces in the cosmos. Energy healers act as a channel or conduit, and through Love can direct this Light energy into themselves and others, but in fact *anyone is capable of accessing the energy* given sufficient loving intention and focus. These powerful energies strengthen your energy chakras and immune system, thus facilitating the body's ability to self-heal in future. In his chapter, Raphael advises on healing yourself and your loved ones. However, always remember *to be effective in helping with the healing of anyone* *else you must first self heal enough to have reached an appropriate level of harmony and balance.*

Now try invoking Raphael to train your "clair" senses to feel his energy:

- *Raphael, Raphael, Raphael, please help with knowledge of what I need for healing and wholeness in mind, body and spirit in Love and Light, Love and Light, Love and Light.*

- *Raphael, Raphael, Raphael, I wish to further my Dance of Six and Five; please help me with this, for my Highest Good.*

Raphael says: *My Key Words are* **HEALING ENERGY SCIENCE, KNOWLEDGE AND MASCULINE ENERGY BALANCE***; with me you can increase your knowledge of the healing power of energy and your own awareness of what you need to address in yourself: This is Energy Science. Plus having gained that knowledge, you will build the willpower to tackle health issues and make decisions.*

To add focus with Raphael, especially on Sundays, the day he rules, you can use:

- A white or yellow candle, or even a gold candle (and this adds Sun and Fire also)
- Raphael's metal is gold (of any carat!) His main crystals are clear quartz or diamond, but as mentioned already you can also use golden or yellow stones such as goldstone, sunstone, topaz and citrine.

Essential oils, although in this section we major on the solar – Raphael's own chakra – as Patron of Healing he of course aids us with all chakras; here is a summary of the seven major chakras with helpful oils, for reference:

Root: Bodily strength, self-esteem and self-respect, survival, forgiveness. This energy centre represents earth and your secure foundations on which to build, all linking to Camael.

General: Patchouli or rosewood. Thyme* is for courage.

Sacral: Innovation, transformation, creativity, sexuality, sensuality.

General: Sandalwood or benzoin; pine for creativity.

Solar: Power of will and mind, decision and action, self-control.

This is Raphael's own chakra, so linked to Creation

Gold and Yellow

General: Ylang ylang, lime, plus ginger for stimulation to action.

Heart: Love including self-love, compassion, surrender, acceptance.

As you know from Haniel's chapter, this means heart and higher heart

General: Jasmine, rosewood or rose.

Throat: Speaking/hearing personal truth, seeking Absolute/Creator's Truth, all aspects of communication and therefore linked to Michael.

General: Camomile or cypress.

Third Eye: Wisdom, discernment, alleviation of stress, development of spiritual vision including safe psychic development, linked to Zadkiel.

General: Hyacinth, cedar wood and rosemary* for general healing, nutmeg for clearing away old thought patterns.

Crown: Cosmic awareness, increasing spiritual consciousness.

General: Frankincense, neroli, rose, or lavender (Melchisadec) will aid spiritual perception, direction and growth.

Not considered suitable for use during pregnancy; always take care and consult an expert to check if you think you may be pregnant or are trying to become pregnant.

An opening message from Raphael on help with healing

I am the Angel Ruler of the Sun; my life-giving rays flow down through the glorious arc of the sky bringing the potential for life to Earth, and helping to make Earth a fit place for that life to dwell. Accordingly I offer my Creation Gold rays for you to absorb at all levels; why not allow my Sun to chase away the shadows from your life? The simplest way is just to visualise Light of brightest gold pouring over and through your body, banishing dark, negative energy. Let my Light dawn on your problems, and dispel gloomy imaginings. The more you focus on dark thoughts, the more you energise them and you can even attract negativity towards yourself, yet the good news is that the reverse is also true with thoughts of Light! Therefore, please allow my rays in to bring you sunlit health and vigour, and to re-vitalise the logical aspects of your brain and empower you to make new decisions.

Your life can be likened to the passage of my Sun through the seasons – whereabouts are you at present? Whatever the actual time of the year why not work towards a new springtime of possibilities? Work with me and Colours of Creation. You can choose to harness the power of my rays; bringing the aspirations you determined with Gabriel into fruition. Then build afresh on this colourful outcome. The Light of my Sun can be split into the Rainbow spectrum, symbols of both me and Melchisadec. You can work with me on physical and emotional energy blocks, and with Melchisadec on etheric healing and spiritual growth. If you are prepared to work with us, our Rainbow spectrum assists the healing and harmony of your body's first seven chakra energy centres. I also aid with Creation Yellow. Later you can move to Sacred Nine adding Turquoise and Magenta, striving through higher vibrations of

White-Gold and White-Silver towards White Fire which derives from the Diamond Rays of Creation. As has been said before, it is all a matter of choice, and appropriate decisions, in which I will always support you with my Love.

Taking a more positive attitude to health

Now we have reached the 21st century people are more conscious than ever before about good nutrition and a healthy lifestyle (even though this knowledge existed with the Zoroastrians!) As mentioned, Raphael is the angel of science and knowledge, and he can be invoked to help you to find the key to your own personal wellbeing which often relates to willpower. The anti-clockwise spiral of the Sun is a Sacred Geometry that will help heal you, if you *will and intend* it to do so.

Raphael's Sun energy strengthens will; as he says:

I am the power of Sun that enlightens and can chase away the shadows. I have told you of Sun healing, but Creation Gold also embodies Creation Yellow; Yellow heals while Gold balances your solar plexus which is where your willpower resides. Try my next exercise; with each breath you take with me, you can strengthen your will a little more. Keep doing this to gradually dispel inner darkness, vulnerability and uncertainty. It will help you heal at all levels, bring greater confidence in your own abilities, and enable you to make decisions that can be life-changing.

Transform with Raphael's Sun and Rainbows! Visualise a bowl of sunlight for optimism at any time it's needed; as Raphael has told you, it will help boost the solar chakra and willpower.

- Imagine you have an invisible bowl filled with blazing golden sunrays in front of you, and that you can hold this bowl in your hands.

- Invoke Raphael and take three deep breaths of this Fire energy, ensuring you breathe it right down into your body and *willing it* to really re-vitalise, for your Highest Good.
- Focus it into your *solar* plexus (*your own Sun centre*); use your will power to visualise this whole area of your body turn to bright yellow gold as your solar chakra absorbs more of this energy and it shines within you.
- Allow Raphael's Light to dawn on any problems. Dark thoughts are banished as you let Sun fill your mind, body, spirit with new vigour, passion and optimism.
- Ask Raphael to help you lock in these benefits with the power of Love and Light
- You can do this quick visualisation as often as you need to lift your spirits, or if you find you are putting off important decisions and/or actions use it until you accomplish your next important step.

A Raphael channelling about achieving Golden (masculine) energy balance: this combines with Yellow of solar chakra, making decisions and taking timely actions.

I travel on a pure Creation Gold spiral that flows anti-clockwise from Father Sun to manifest all life on Mother Earth. It is the glorious energy ray whose nurturing warmth brings you joy of living, banishes darkness and enlightens your life and future. But my real task, as given by the Creator, is to guide you towards expanding your own knowledge of self-healing and harmony. This is energy science, and once you are aware of its potential, you can use this knowledge for self and life and even offer it to help All.

Consider your life as a canvas on which you can create any picture you like. To do this, however, you need good health else your picture will be faint indeed. You also require balance and harmony between the active, Gold aspect of your personality and your passive, Silver side. Gold (your left brain and right side of the body) is the aspect of you that makes decisions, using logic and analytical skills, and takes action accordingly – you could say it is the power of your will and mind. Silver (right brain, left side), links to your feelings, heart's intuition and imagination and is, as you have learnt, ruled by the Moon whose Guardian is Gabriel. That elusive balance of masculine and feminine attributes (regardless of your birth gender) thus requires support from both of us.

If you would receive my solar chakra healing close your eyes and breathe my energy. See spirals of Gold and Yellow travel down through your meridian, circling anti-clockwise into your solar chakra. Absorb as much of this as you can, for apart from the heart (linked to Gabriel's Moon as well as to Haniel) the solar plexus is the place where emotions may have been suppressed. While Gold brings masculine balance to six of your seven chakras, Creation Yellow and Gold will flow together as one into your solar chakra (hence its name!) If you truly want to empower your will and mind to help you grow spiritually, I can help you work towards actually igniting a miniature Sun within this chakra. Then you can harness my power at all, even cellular, levels.

When ready you can return Gold upwards in an anti-clockwise spiral to your left brain (third eye chakra) where it will join with the clockwise Creation Silver energy of Gabriel which touches right brain*.

If, as you heal with each of the Sacred Seven, you also work with our Caduceus in the next exercise using my Creation Gold and Gabriel's Creation Silver, you will gradually balance all of the first six chakras, thus you begin to attain that higher level of harmony you seek. *See Gabriel chapter

Now that you know how to work with both Raphael and Gabriel, to enhance your healing efforts, you can try using the Caduceus symbol as depicted here, which symbolises grounding, integration and polarity balance. The Caduceus of Raphael, also traditionally depicted with Hermes Trismegistus as I mention in Ancient Angel Wisdom, aids the balancing of polarities of six major chakra centres: root, sacral, solar, heart, throat, third eye. Also the Wings are Wisdom of Air – the higher self and Above, harmonising with Wisdom of Earth – lower self and Below. In Sanscrit this is called "sushumna" – the staff, and ida and pingala are the twin rays.

Caduceus exercise for both Gold/Solar and Silver/Lunar energy balance

- Make a pyramid shape above your head by joining your two palms, pointing upwards.
- Invoke Raphael and Gabriel, asking them to join you from Sun and Sky: All Above, to Earth and Moon: All Below.
- They do this by placing the Caduceus into the third eye and your meridian and firmly down into Mother Earth.
- Ask that the Caduceus links you with the crystal heart of Mother Earth where the Sacred Earth Flame burns.
- Become a conduit to allow Sun's Creation Gold and Moon's Creation Silver energies to flow down the Caduceus until they reach and are renewed in the Sacred Earth Flame.
- Then visualise the twin Gold/Solar (anti-clockwise) and Silver/Lunar (clockwise) energies, personified by gold and silver snakes of wisdom, wind back up the caduceus, balancing your polarities by crossing in each of the six chakras in turn, beginning with the root and ending at third eye:
- As they do so, say: *I seek grounding, integration and polarity balance of Sun and Moon to the third eye, to move towards Crown and Oneness. I ask as these energies meet and cross:*

- *Left and Right,*
- *Silver and Gold,*
- *Raphael and Gabriel*
- *Masculine and Feminine,*
- *Sun and Moon*
- *Ida and Pingala (Sanscrit)*

- At this point they will have reached and met just above your third eye chakra.
- Then bring down your palms and thank the angels for their help; some say "Namaste" to honour the East.
- When you have attained the right level of self-healing, harmony and balance and are ready to move into Oneness with All, you will start to feel a higher level of energy balance (white-gold and white-silver), as the angel wings show you are preparing to move out of polarity and to crown chakra and White Fire.

Energy healing and addressing "The wounded healer (Chiron)"

As mentioned before, Raphael, patron angel of healers, was given responsibility by the Creator for making the earth a fit place for life and for aiding the healing of man. He is guardian of the sacred knowledge, or science of healing, and therefore when we work closely with him, he makes it possible for us to develop a fuller understanding of our own wonderful powers of recovery.

If you resonate strongly with Raphael, it suggests you have an inherent healing skill that you should develop. You may, however, need some self-healing first, most of us do, because the stressful process of life at the current vibration depletes energy levels, so that we must continually re-balance this energy to maintain good health.

Life force energy, also called Universal Source, is the Love and

Light gift of Spirit – White Fire Angelic Light, containing within all rainbow colours and devolving, in this reality, from the Diamond Ray of the Seraphim Creation Angels. White Fire is also called the Quintessence and holds the purest (White) vibrations of Earth, Air – Breath of Life, and Water of Life. Ask Raphael how you can learn to channel this to first strengthen your immune system, thus enhancing the body's self-healing ability, and sealing it in with his Creation Gold through all chakras.

If you genuinely desire to give healing to others, you must strive to be centred and whole yourself, for in a mystical process the healing creates a synergy between healer and healee allowing beneficial Love and Angelic Light to flow between.

A visualisation to help develop energy healing ability

Try this visualisation with Raphael; you can work with him to help develop, or enhance, your own healing skills that you can apply to self and others. The more your heart wishes you to use them, the stronger they will become. You can ask for Raphael's connective Attunement in this meditation

- Close your eyes and start taking deep breaths of pure white energy, breathing out any negative emotions, until you start to feel relaxed.
- Then invoke Raphael like this: *Raphael, Raphael, Raphael, I ask for your connective Angelic Light Attunement of Sun so that I can self-heal.*
- Optionally also say: *I breathe in Creation Gold of your Sun to flow into me, empowering me to first heal self and then aid others to heal; fill me with your power of Love and Light, for the Highest Good of All.*
- Now imagine that you can take a deep breath in of this life-giving energy.
- Breathe it into your body, expanding it with heart and then grounding it in Mother Earth; bring it back to visualise

Creation Gold rays forming a miniature Sun in your solar plexus chakra.

- Keep breathing in Raphael's golden energy to your own miniature Sun and radiating rays throughout your lower body, particularly to boost the power of your will and intention to heal.
- Then, as you breathe out say: *With Raphael I breathe a Yellow-Gold Healing Star from my own Sun in my solar chakra, out into my aura.*
- You should be able to feel or even see this energy within as well as around you, and as it is Fire energy it will be tingling or sparkling and you can draw on it.
- Optionally you can now say: *Raphael: I inform the Universe with this Star that from now on I pledge to heal self as well as using this healing Sun energy to aid others with healing.*
- It depends on how often you think about it as to how long the Sun and Star will last and whether you keep sending this out to help heal All. It is likely to last between 36 and 48 hours, after which you may need to re-create it. The main thing is to use it! If you create and use it frequently it may become permanent.
- You can do this exercise as often as you need to ask for Raphael's loving assistance to help to heal your life and help loved ones as well.
- Don't forget to thank him!

Wishing on a crystal for health (or to encapsulate specific healing requests)

You can use any Raphael crystal for this, (and you could even programme a diamond ring!) Also angelite, celestite and angel hair quartz would be particularly appropriate.

- Choose a small crystal that will fit into the centre of your palm, or wear it.

- Preferably have this in or on your left (taking) hand, deciding in your mind on a suitable wish; to work this must be something for your Highest Good.
- Then invoke Raphael in the normal way, asking for support for health and wellbeing three times over your chosen crystal adding the words: in Love and Light, Love and Light, Love and Light.
- Finally with your right palm or hand push your wish into the crystal until your two hands are closed together, and your wish or request is then encapsulated.
- Whenever you view it, remind yourself to focus on this energy request, or else give it to someone else who needs special healing, with instructions to focus.

The Place of Rainbows: a full healing meditation for the seven major chakras

This powerful meditation will enable you to receive some healing in all seven major chakra energy centres of your body, and into your aura, engendering peace and relaxation and increasing your overall sense of health, harmony and wellbeing. You could record it to listen to, but you don't have to do it exactly like this. You can read it three times to get a feel of what happens, and just begin the meditation, reach the crystal pyramid, and see what unfolds for you, letting the angels take charge.

- Ensure you are comfortable, warm and undisturbed for approximately thirty minutes. Relax, detach, centre and focus within yourself. Take some deep, calming breaths and invoke Raphael, asking him to be with you for your Highest Good. Send roots from your feet into Mother Earth so that you are grounded and open up your energy chakras, visualising their colours. For this it helps to see them as a series of appropriately coloured flowers (*see also*

140

Harmony Angel Cards or Angel Quest of the Heart)

- Draw down Sun energy with Raphael, through the crown, anti-clockwise, feeling it travelling down through each chakra until it reaches the base. Then feel it go down your legs and reach your toes. Send it through the roots in your feet into Mother Earth's heart, for grounding, ask for healing to be directed through her around the world and then re-link back to Raphael.

- Now bring your focus back and imagine yourself standing high on a sacred mound or hill. All around you is breath-taking scenery; you marvel at the work of the Creator. The air is cool and invigorating; breathe deeply of it.

- Below you see a grove of trees. You walk down the side of the hill until you reach the calming blue shade of the trees. You enter the grove of trees and immediately you become part of the stillness and quiet atmosphere; the trees symbolise your grounding, your roots and your potential for growth.

- Emerging from the trees, you feel the warm healing sun on your face. In front of you is a huge crystal pyramid, and as the sun strikes it, glorious rainbows are formed; feel the energy generated by Sacred Seven Creation Colours.

- The Rainbow angels Raphael and Melchisadec are waiting beside the pyramid, one each side of a triangular door.

- They beckon you forward and presently you stand in front of the pyramid itself.

- The door in the pyramid slides open allowing you to enter, closing behind you. In the centre of the pyramid is a crystal fountain, filled with myriad Light Rainbows. As you stand in front of this fountain call on the angels for rainbow healing, in Love and Light, Love and Light, Love and Light.

- The fountain leaps up and seems to flow all around you. Feel the appropriate colour ray enter each chakra until all seven flowers glow with dazzling light. Now imagine the colours radiating outwards into your aura, symbols of health and vitality. Feel your aura sparkling with clearer colours.

- Request that Raphael seals in the healing with the Creation Gold of his Sun; rays flow in through the top point of the pyramid and bathe you in Gold, until your inner and outer body glows with a golden radiance.
- Ask the angels to bring you back to your physical body. Look within yourself to examine the chakra centres, which should be brighter in colour.
- Breathe deeply three times to ground yourself and return to normal consciousness.
- If you wish you can mentally seal each chakra flower with a golden Sun sphere, and don't forget to thank Raphael and Melchisadec for their help.

Angels have been helping us with healing since the dawn of Time

The knowledge of energy healing dates back thousands of years. Raphael was also equated with Thoth/Hermes Trismegistus, a being originally Atlantean, then Egyptian and later absorbed into the Greek pantheon, who was credited with bringing healing, astronomy, sacred geometry, science and much other wisdom to man. However, in fact these are two completely different angels.

The sacred symbol that has been traditionally associated with both Raphael and Thoth/Hermes is the Caduceus, used to symbolise medical knowledge and to heal to third eye level, for as I have said, beyond this, the crown chakra denotes moving into Oneness. Raphael is traditionally tasked with the healing of Mother Earth and mankind in this reality but both Raphael and Hermes Trismegistus are concerned with ancient wisdom to aid our Gold/Solar and our Silver/Lunar balance. Where Raphael works in conjunction with Gabriel, as you now know, Hermes Trismegistus works in conjunction with Pistis Sophia – Mother of the Zodiac Angels and links us through the Zodiac Gateways to harmony and beyond, towards other realities.

Archaeologists believe that both crystals and oils were used to enhance healing in Ancient Egypt. Carnation, frankincense, narcissus, hyacinth and rose are all fragrances that will help to "call" angels to you by bringing them closer. This is because they are said to resemble perfumes in the angelic realms themselves. You can either burn a candle perfumed with one of these, or a few drops of essential oil mixed with water in an oil burner, to enhance your ability to communicate with your chosen and/or Primary Guardian Angel.

Angels' Wings and Feathers

Angels are also known as The Shining Ones. When you find a white feather, or particularly if you find three white feathers in succession – following the Law of Three of Hermes Trismegistus, the angels are definitely telling you that your focus should turn to spirituality and further spiritual development. Or if you happen to be thinking of something: a talk, a course, a book, or something similar, that will specifically bring spiritual direction or growth, and a white feather floats by *at that moment, then the angels are confirming this step is definitely right for you.*

Although I stopped collecting tiny white feathers years ago, preferring to leave them for others to find, this latter sign happens to me all the time, even after fifteen years. It occurs frequently when I am thinking about a new book or angel course to write, confirming I am on the right track. Wherever we have reached on the Way of Love & Light there are always new beginnings offered, and in spiritual terms they will be at the next, higher level. This is what the Five Point Star (Dance of Five) really means. It's about our perpetual struggle to reach those

higher levels until we attain a perfection of heart and soul (as with Ascended Masters). At this point we would no longer *have* to incarnate again; but we could nevertheless *choose* to do so, to aid the living to find the Way.

The Three Spheres (Tiers or Hierarchies) of Angels

There are Three Spheres of Angels, each containing a Triad (three groups). At the top, closest to the Creator, are Seraphim, Cherubim and Thrones. The second Triad is Dominions, Powers and Virtues. The third Triad, traditionally nearest mankind, comprises Angel Princes (or Principalities), Archangels and Angels. It is written that these nine groups' attributes encompass all qualities or virtues of the Creator, and to which mankind should therefore aspire.

Once it was thought mankind could only communicate with Angels and Archangels from the lowest Triad, and indeed, perhaps that was the case. Since 2000, however, and following various heavenly conjunctions (Grand Crosses, Six Point Star configurations etc.) and the large number of healers sending out Love & Light to All, we have raised our own and the planetary vibration. I believe that if we will and intend to open our higher hearts to Love, we immediately connect with the Angelic Light vibration of *all three groups in the first Triad*: Angels, Archangels, Angel Princes.

Further choices await us. If we continue to work daily with angels to raise our own vibration, this will enable us to connect with the second Sphere and Triad. Following on from there, if we also work to aid others, transitioning from our own Heart Quest and self-healing to Soul Quest, in which we aid Mother Earth and All Life to heal, I know and have proved in my books and teachings that we are able to connect and work with the highest

Sphere and Triad, in other words, even with the Seraphim. These are the Creation Angels who were there at the birth of mankind, and who were immensely saddened at the "Falls", but who are joyfully guiding our re-Ascension; theirs is the Diamond Ray and Dodecahedron (Platonic Solid of Spirit).

It is really just a question of free will, of deciding to combine our open heart flower with an intention guided by Love, Beauty and Compassion and a desire from soul to be in Oneness with All; *if our heart's and soul's desire is to do this, then we can.*

The Seven Musical Notes of the first Seven Major Chakras

Each of the first seven major chakras traditionally has a musical note and sound vibration, and you can use this vibration to help with energy balance. This is the general consensus of the chakra notes, though as you develop spiritually the notes also can become more refined.

C is for the Root Chakra
D is for the Sacral
E is for the Solar
F is for the Heart
G is for the Throat
A is for the Third Eye
B is for the Crown

And this brings us neatly back to the final chapter of this book: Melchisadec – Ruler of Seven in all its sacred and alchemical aspects.

Chapter Eleven

Melchisadec and his Seventh Violet Ray
of Alchemy

Melchisadec's Key Words: Rainbow (linked to Sacred Seven and the first Seven Rainbow Colours of Creation), Chalice containing Key to the heart of the Seven-Turn Labyrinth. All of these key words relate to spiritual fast-tracking through finding your true self and are facilitated by Melchisadec's Creation Violet Ray of Alchemy.

Now that you have worked with his Sacred Seven, Melchisadec summarises what you may have accomplished and offers you a more advanced channelling to study:

You now must learn that there are different levels of vibration to attain with me. Working with me and my Sacred Seven is a powerful, spiritual new beginning and I have guided you through this. Together with Raphael I have taught you about Rainbows and the power of Love and Light. You took your first Angelology steps to heal towards wholeness, peace, Oneness. As you now know, mine is the magical power of Seven, and the Seventh – Violet – Ray that transmutes illusion, lighting the labyrinthine way to your heart centre. For remember, I hold the Chalice or Grail – your quest to find your soul purpose.

Those are my symbols, and the path I teach is the Rainbow Path to the centre of my Seven-turn Labyrinth: place of inner peace. While you still have much to learn, and some of the ultimate Twelve Creation Colours to fully comprehend, I hope your path to find your own true self is now becoming clearer. To further aid this clarity it is time to work with my own Creation Violet, especially on third eye chakra, building on what you learnt with Michael and Zadkiel and bringing my angelic alchemy into your life.

As I wrote in the first part of this book, Creation Violet is born of Melchisadec's magical Seventh Ray. If a bright, pure and clear Violet pulses as a kind of sphere in your third eye, as it has done with me since all this began in 1999, and with many other readers and students drawn to study with me, it signifies that you have belonged in a past life to the Melchisadec Order (Order of Melchizedek or the Great White Brotherhood). You will have had the power to work with many aspects of the Ray which links also with Ariel, Ruler of Earth and Air, the Nature Angel Guardians, as well as Michael and Divine Truth. If you have not already done so, when the time is right you can and will retrieve this power, which resides always in a level of your spiritual consciousness.

Depending on where you are on The Way of Love & Light and with your self-healing (Heart Quest) and aiding others to heal (your Soul Quest), the shades of Violet will subtly multiply. When you view through the eye of heart and higher heart chakra, you will perceive these variations as well as intuit their uses. Deep Violet-Purple links with Earth and grounding. Fire aspects are hot, Water aspects are cool. Warm shades are red-purple, violet-magenta, crimson or rose-violet. The cooler shades are bluish: deep indigo through blue-purple, blue-violet, lavender (Air). Spiritual shades are pale, rose-gold-violet and silver-blue-violet. If you are only able to see one shade at present, don't worry as this will change when you are ready to move on to the subtle variations of the colour; there are many levels of Violet Ray Angelic Light Attunements that can be received or retrieved; contact me to find out more on this.

Adding focus with Melchisadec's special crystals and oils

Crystals: Rainbow quartz and rainbow obsidian, amethyst for the Violet Ray, sugilite or sodalite. You could use Diamond: also the crystal of the Seraphim Creation Angels. Oils: Lavender oil is always good; frankincense and myrrh are very spiritual.

Working with the Violet Ray of Creation

Some simple ways of working with the Seventh Ray – Creation Violet – for general cleansing, whether externally or within self.

As Melchisadec says: *Violet embodies a form of alchemy: it is the spiritual antiseptic that can transmute all dark energy, returning it to pure White Light. Use it in the ways I suggest. You can dispel darkness, in my name, calling forth the power of Violet as healing spirals and drawing them around or within self, willing and intending from heart with Love for negativity to be dissipated.*

- To clear a room after harsh words have been said or violent actions have taken place (usually a cool Creation Violet shade is needed).

  - After an argument you can cleanse the room by simply invoking Melchisadec, calling his name Sacred Seven times, and then saying: *please cleanse this room with Creation Violet, in love and light, love and light, love and light.* Visualise violet spirals absorbing the dark energy. You should actually be able to feel the atmosphere in the room become lighter. Remember to thank him!

- If you are going into what you *know* will be a very negative situation with someone.

- Adapt the above invocation by holding a small amethyst crystal in your left hand and saying: *Melchisadec, Melchisadec, Melchisadec please help me use this crystal to transmute the negative atmosphere I am entering, for my highest good.* Breathe in cool Violet spirals; breathing them out into the crystal, then sealing them in with right hand. Carry the crystal until your meeting or task is finished; later cleanse it three times in cold running water or place overnight under a full moon to clear with Gabriel's Creation Silver.

- To cleanse a room that seems to have a negative energy stuck in it from something that happened in the past (usually do this with a hot Violet shade).

  - Place an amethyst or other suitable crystal in each corner and then use Melchisadec's great power of Sacred Seven with Sacred Sound. To do this you sing out loud "Melchisadec Hallelujah" seven times, while walking around the room. This brings in healing, usually via a hot, purifying vibration of Creation Violet in Melchisadec's name, therefore it is very effective. If I move house I always do this in each and every room of the new dwelling, several times if necessary!

You can now try using Melchisadec's Violet Ray quickly yet more subtly if you sometimes suddenly need to counteract extremes of emotion.

If you could "see" blocks of negative emotions such as fear, sorrow, anger or frustration in your chakras, you could see these also appear as dark patches of energy in your aura. At any time you can ask from your heart for Melchisadec to bring you an invisible but very effective bowl of Creation Violet flames. If you feel you have this negativity within, perhaps from a quarrel, you can instantly call up amazing energy by saying:

Melchisadec, Melchisadec, Melchisadec please bring me a bowl of your Creation Violet Rays for my Highest Good.

- Now visualise a wide yet shallow bowl in front of you, filled to the brim with dancing Creation Violet. (You may see either one, or several shades of Violet.)

- There are two ways of using this bowl:
  - Take a deep breath and breathe into your cupped hands the negative emotion from within you that you want to immediately transmute.
  - Imagine that you now hold this dark energy within your cupped hands and simply "throw" it into the invisible bowl using your loving will and intention to transmute it. The dark energy will instantly disappear, and if you have the visual "clair" skills, you may see white sparkles in the Violet.
  - "Know" that this has taken place, and then you can always ask Melchisadec and Raphael for healing support in terms of any replenishing Colours of Creation you need.

- Using the bowl in reverse:
  - You can also visualise the bowl and breathe in alchemy of Violet Rays to counteract and cleanse away negativity from a sudden situation that has made you feel angry, frightened, upset or despairing. We will build on this further in the chapter, with more intense visualisations.

Moving on to focus on the important task of transmuting

outdated mind-sets:

Alchemy: a self-transforming Spiritual Alchemy Ritual for the third eye chakra

You can take advantage of this spiritual alchemy in a more struc-
tured way, as offered by this Ritual. Use it to rid yourself of old
mind-sets, as well as the negative behavioural patterns they
cause to repeat in your life. This is with Melchisadec and adds
other angels of Violet like Ariel (Ruler of Earth & Air) and
Aratron (Guardian of Nature Magic). Some readers will also be
aware that Ascended Master, St. Germain is connected with the
Violet Ray and can be invoked in this Ritual. Because Creation
Violet connects directly with the third eye, you can focus it
specifically *in this chakra* to transmute the negative energy of
those stubborn mindsets; take care, however, not to allow them
back in! This leaves you free to re-programme yourself for the
future.

- **Optionally:** Set up your ritual with a violet cloth and
  candle, and an amethyst or other Melchisadec crystal.
  Anoint the violet candle with a drop of lavender (or frankincense oil if you have it) and light it.

- **Now:** Write down on a piece of paper those repeating
  behavioural habits, mind-sets or thought patterns that you
  wish to transmute; you can even address blocks or ties that
  you feel may be from other lifetimes.

- **Next:** Speak the following: *"Melchisadec, in the name of your
  Seventh Ray and the alchemy it holds, I call you forth, with
  Aratron (Nature Magic), Ariel (Ruler of Earth/Air), St.
  Germain and all Creation Violet energies in Love and Light,
  Love and Light, Love and Light. I ask to use this Violet in the
  vibration I need to set myself free from old mind-sets, habits or*

behavioural patterns from the past, in order to allow new psychic skills to develop, for my Highest Good"

- **When** you have said the final sentence breathe in the Creation Violet that you need and bring this into your crown chakra; it travels down to the third eye chakra, really will and intend the thorough purifying of the third eye chakra. Keep doing this until you sense it becoming cleansed and transformed into a brighter shade (or shades) of Violet. Then you will have rebalanced and re-empowered the third eye.

- **Next:** Thank the Beings for their loving assistance, burn the piece of paper on which you wrote earlier, ensuring it reduces completely to ash.

- **Finally:** When only ash remains, to mentally and physi-cally draw a line under the image you had of your old self, *bury the ash in the ground and ensure you dwell no more on it: for you are now ready to move on.*

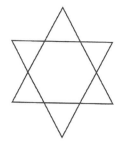

A Six Point Star Meditation for Seven-fold Violet Cleansing: to be able to expand your psychic ability in the third eye chakra

Invoke Melchisadec to be with you in the usual way, and I advise you to invoke Raphael's and Gabriel's presence also.

Read through this whole visualisation before you begin including the footnote. Then:

- Take some deep breaths in and out of pure, sparkling white Spiritus Dei energy expelling any and all negative thoughts, until you feel filled with Light.

- Ground this energy through your feet, sending it to down to Mother Earth to link to her crystal heart, then to Gabriel's Moon, and finally to All Below.

- Bring energy back through your feet, sending it through your crown to Raphael's Sun and on to All Above.

- Now you are held for a short while in the Creation Gold and Silver energies, while you do this important spiritual exercise.

- Visualise yourself standing inside Melchisadec's Six-Pointed Star of Macrocosm, remember this is a symbol of your true connection to All That Exists.**

  - One at a time you will take SIX special Creation Violet cleansing and transmuting breaths, (one for each of the star points)

  - With each in-breath say the words *"Melchisadec, Melchisadec, Melchisadec let Love and your Creation Violet Light flow into me."*

  - With each out-breath say *"I am ready to release more negative energy blocks; please let them be transmuted into White Fire."*

  - *Really will and intend this to happen!*

- Now you are ready to breathe the final, powerful Seventh Violet breath to work some spiritual alchemy.

- As you breathe in this final breath of Violet Ray say: *Melchisadec please allow my heart to receive your connective Angelic Light Attunement with its gift of spiritual alchemy, in Love and Light, Love and Light, Love and Light.*

- Spend a few moments in this sacred space, in your heart, enjoying the energy connection you have made to mighty Melchisadec and sending this alchemical energy to flow from heart both to lower self and also to higher self.

- Now say: *I also wish to safely build higher psychic ("clair") skills in my third eye chakra, if for my Highest Good and the*

Highest Good of All. Please allow me to become a clear channel for Creation Violet to help heal mankind, Mother Earth and All Life.

- When you are ready to conclude, ask Raphael and Gabriel to seal in all the healing with their gold and silver rays of harmony and balance.
- You can do this visualisation as many times as necessary to release more blocks and/or to become more adept at channelling Creation Violet.
- Remember to send all the angels Love, Light and thanks in return.

**In two-dimensional format the six points of the Macrocosm Star represent six major chakras, with the seventh, central point being your heart. See Star above. This is how we begin with this sacred geometry and Dance of Six; later in this chapter there is more on this vis-a-vis your Dance of Six and Five. In three-dimensional format this Star becomes a Star Tetrahedron as Seven becomes Nine, itself a preparation for Twelve etc. Also see Part Three of Angel Almanac for more on this and it is also taught in my e-Mystery Courses: Ascension with Angels and Awakening the Crystalline Heart)

Moving on to use Creation Violet Rays in different types of healing

Melchisadec speaks on self-transformation and how Creation Violet truly helps you to experience spiritual alchemy; here is his message to you at this point:

I, Melchisadec, ruler of Sacred Seven, counsel you now to consider the true, arcane significance of this in your own healing. You began healing seven main chakra energy centres, all of which need to function correctly for wholeness in mind, body and spirit before you can move on. Although there are always more levels of healing in the Dance of Six to address in order to be able to raise your vibration further on your Dance of Five, you have begun to empower third eye chakra and to develop your own psychic awareness.

You should now be able to trace a seven-fold path (my Labyrinth) through your body to analyse where any problems still lie. You will have released many blocks now, but sometimes deeper ones then appear from past lives. Depending on the nature of those remaining blocks, you also know from the previous Violet cleansing visualisations, that you can add Violet Ray breaths or do transmutation exercises with Violet when working more with my Sacred Seven and their attributes. This is especially useful if you have got to deeper third eye blocks caused by mind-sets that you now need to remove, often from many lifetimes ago.

Moving on from this, if you have thoroughly cleansed and healed with my own Violet Ray, as well as used the healing geometry of my Six-Point Star of Macrocosm, you can then let more Light in; it will blaze forth to guide your way to my Labyrinth (See graphic below).

My seven-turn labyrinth is a symbol of the route to find that physical and spiritual harmony that I spoke of at the beginning of this book. In fact this whole book has all been part of the labyrinthine path to your true self. If you have committed to this work with me and my Sacred Seven, I will also help you find the courage to walk the Labyrinth to its very centre: a key part of your Heart  *Quest path of harmony and completion, so long as when you have found your own inner peace, you move on to your Soul Quest and lead others on this Way.*

Remember Creation Violet Light contains pink and blue – more pink (Love) from the opening heart makes warm violet that impassions, while more blue is cool violet that speaks of Truth, the paler the colour the higher the Truth. Silvery, lavender-blue violet is a very spiritual shade, as it is Breath of Life. Rose-gold-violet means more compassion.

You have reached the point now where you are ready to learn more about your own Sacred Geometry Dance of Six and Five. Melchisadec enlightens you:

In Angelic Numerology all numbers are important and bring you messages from us. If you are seeing 77, 777 or 77:77 then you are an ancient soul and Sacred Seven is the key if you are to retrieve your own ancient wisdom.

I wish to instruct you a little more now on your Dance of Six and Five, for it is vital to your spiritual fast-tracking. As you are already aware, in two dimensional terms mine is the Six-Point Star of Macrocosm: All

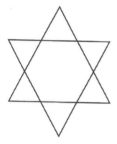

That Is – healed, whole and complete. The interlocking triangle comprises Earth, Air, Water and Fire but most important of all is my invisible seventh central point. There also Spirit –the Quintessence or 5th Element can be said to reside, and this is the point of Alchemy. You have used this Star in an exercise, and know it represents you and your first seven major chakra energy centres (your heart is the centre point, corresponding to Quintessence, because through heart is your spiritual consciousness raised). As you have learnt (and hopefully now experienced) each time you accomplish a new level of self-healing you reach a new level of vibration, in other words a brand new level of your Dance of Six. I hope you have now worked to reach that new stage because then you, who are Man the Microcosm, will have earned a chance to further expand your spiritual consciousness via your Dance of Five.

Here below is the symbol of your Dance of Five: the Five-Point Star. This Sacred Geometry Star, in two dimensional form, stands for Man the Microcosm. Its top-most point is your crown, while the other four points are your limbs.

It is a message about the Five vibration. The top point stretches towards God/The Creator via us, the Messengers, and therefore it represents your spiritual quest, that is until you reach perfection in soul. Every time you strive to achieve some self-healing on the Six vibration level (your Dance of Six), you will be offered the chance to attain a new level of spirituality on the Five vibration (your Dance of Five). In turn, that prepares you for a new level of healing on the Six vibration, and so on. It is a spiritual Dance between the numbers, and through the Colours of Creation – taking you from Seven to Nine and then through higher Gold and higher Silver. Then with Twelve you reach White Fire Angelic Light – the pure Light of Spirit on your Earth beyond which is Diamond of the Creation Angels. Finally there is Thirteen – Twelve around One; this is the higher Dance of Twelve and Thirteen and a whole new programme unfolds for you.*

All this while, the more spiritually developed you become, the closer you will draw to us, the angels, and to the Creator; the ultimate goal being to move out of the polarity of your "Fallen" reality Below and to return to be with us Above, in Oneness, even holding that Ascension connection through heart for All.

It is perfectly possible now for you to attain the ultimate spiritual goal of bringing Heaven to Earth (As Below So Above). And as you discover that sacred geometry is the Universal pattern of cosmic Spirit, and absorb a little of that mystery unto yourself in your Dance, becoming part of that sacred geometry, your spiritual consciousness will continue to grow. This is a vertical expansion into what you term Space. You become taller and taller; and I can definitely assure you the Sky is not the limit where spirituality is concerned!

Now you have learnt a little more about the Seventh Ray of Violet, and if you have worked with each angel in the book you will have developed connections with Melchisadec and all of his

Sacred Seven. You could take this opportunity to obtain further guidance from Melchisadec on whether you are ready for more spiritual fast-tracking. While doing these meditations you can pause and go into your heart. There you can safely ask Melchisadec for direct guidance, using your new "clair" skills. You may hear words or intuit (an "inner knowing") about your own next step on your Dance of Six and Five. The more healing you channel, the more guidance you will receive.

How to *begin to be* a Light Worker with Melchisadec, Sacred Seven and Violet

If you feel drawn to do this, you have already begun by requesting to be a clear channel in the Six Point Star Meditation. Now you can try using your new ability to create and send Creation Violet energy rays to heal and transmute blocks in others. You can send this wonderful energy to individuals, groups, countries and places where natural disasters or wars occur, as well as to the fabric of Earth, her Nature Kingdom, her seas, waters and atmosphere.

- Sit quietly in a chair and focus on your third eye and crown.
- Take some deep, relaxing breaths and ask Raphael to surround you with the golden healing energy of his Sun.
- Focus on the energy meridian within you and open all the chakras.
- Breathe Raphael's Sun energy through the meridian and ground it in Earth.
- Bring through Gabriel's Moon energy from Earth and link to Sun, thus you are held in these protective energies yet link your own meridian to theirs.
- Consider the colour of Creation Violet you need, or leave this to the angels!

- Breathe Creation Violet into your crown chakra, bring it down into the third eye chakra. As you do this, form it into a ball; it starts about the size of a tennis ball.
- Focus on the fact that you are asking for this energy to give healing and love to others and/or Mother Earth herself.
- Take the Violet energy ball down through the throat to the heart; visualise it growing with each chakra, and as it reaches the heart expand it with Love.
- Feel it travel down gathering more energy and expanding until it reaches your root chakra, by which time it will be at least the size of a football!
- Tell Melchisadec you wish him to help you send this energy to *whomever or whatever cause you have chosen*, and ask the angels to help it to be received for the Highest Good.
- Bring it back to the heart and imagine it can exit from your heart. Catch it between your two palms. You will probably be able to actually feel the energy ball within your hands. Amazing but most people can!
- To send it, slowly and very gradually begin to close your hands together. You will actually feel the Violet Energy Ball compress.
- As you bring your palms slowly together, say out loud "*I send this healing in Love, Peace and Light, Love, Power and Wisdom and the greatest of these is Love*". The moment you close your two palms together (in prayer position) the Violet Energy Ball is sent and you will no longer feel it. (You created and sent it in the 4th Dimension)
- Remember to thank all the angels who helped you create this!
- This can also be used just to send healing energy Above and Below.
- Even more powerful as a group exercise.

More Angelic Wisdom on Melchisadec

Melchisadec can also be spelt Melchizedek. Why do spellings of angel names vary? Because in the days before parchment, when papyrus was used, this crumbled after a certain time so scribes had to copy and recopy the texts with the angels' names. They were also re-copied as they were translated over the centuries. This gave rise to small variations of the same names appearing. For example, Zadkiel sometimes appears as Sachiel or Tsadkiel. Even if the spelling differs slightly, the sound vibration, and thus the sacred energy, remains the same. I regard the spelling I use for Melchisadec as more feminine, and the other spelling – Melchizedek as masculine, although as I mentioned before, angels have no need of genders!

A concluding channelling from Melchisadec

This is about further spiritual advancement and fast-tracking

You have now accomplished much, and you may choose to remain at this point; if you do so and send out healing energy you will greatly help us, the Angels of Love & Light. Yet, from this point, and if your choice is to go further with me, I can guide the journey of your self-healing. In this regard I counsel you that in tandem with physical progression, I shall lead you to advanced spiritual development; you may be sure the one supports the other if you seek my pure Harmonic of Light.

To facilitate your harmony quest you can use my teachings in your life in as many ways as possible, to commune with your subconscious and engender even greater progress. With my Sacred Seven, on your self-healing Heart Quest, you have begun to heal a level of mind, body and spirit with some of the Twelve Colours of Creation, working through the spectrum as your journey commences. It has been mentioned that if you continue to Sacred Nine and then to Twelve (and Thirteen), you have reached Oneness.

If you wish to advance further on the spiritual path with me, into

Soul Quest, with a view to aiding others, you return to work at higher levels with my Rainbow and Sacred Nine (three groups of three chakras, multi-dimensional sacred geometry) and so forth. You will find that as the vibration rises, each colour you work with will gradually become paler, more refined. Colours will appear opalescent and pearly to those of you who are ancient souls and who have worked with the Colours of Creation in past lives. It depends on your personal origins as to what power you will retrieve. You may have been Atlantean or Lemurian, or even Star Born: a wise soul from another galaxy. If you are drawn to me and Violet you will certainly have been in the Great White Brotherhood which is also called the Order of Melchisadec.

But your origins – even your past lives – matter not, except in healing terms. What is important is that you retrieve your own wisdom and redevelop your ability to work now with any or all of these higher vibrations (Light Codes) of the Colours. And even more importantly, that you help us, the angels, by channelling, grounding and manifesting these subtle energies for us, magnifying them in your own heart before sending them out to All; especially with my own Violet Rays of healing.

If, or when, you awaken your Crystalline Heart you are helping to channel White Fire - my pure Harmonic of Light (known as Angelic or Metatronic Light) as well as to send this out as healing Sacred Geometry fractals. This is what you term Heart Ascension and when enough of this energy is created to bathe your planet and all its sentient life forms, White Fire given form by your Love, you will help us to help you bring about full Planetary Ascension. In other words, you make a positive contribution to return your Earth to her original pure vibration – the one she occupied before your various falls from Grace. This whole process has begun to happen; for since your linear year of December 2012 you are in what is called the "Quickening".

Will you help us, the angels of Love and Light, to aid you with this? Much has been hidden from you for thousands of years, including your own true origins, other dimensions and other realities and worlds, yet

161

as we lift those veils on the Mysteries in your "now" there is much, much more that you can experience through your expanding psychic ("clair") senses.

As you read my words, you are truly at a wonderful, potential new beginning. I call on you: Man the Microcosm, to reach up to touch Spirit, so that we, the angels, can now reach down to touch you. Throughout this book we have enabled you to make this connection permanent. Once I came through your sister Planet Venus to incarnate among you, to sew the seeds of Love and Light for this time on your Earth. If you invoke me now, I manifest in my true energy form to facilitate your spiritual journey; my task is to remain until your Planetary Ascension – your endgame – is attained. You can play a role in this, small or large, if you continue working with me and other angels, although the further you travel along the Way of Love & Light, the more you will realise that in wisdom terms it is but another new beginning: the adventure continues in Time and Space. Whatever level of assistance you pledge, in exponential ways it benefits All, and however you choose to participate I bid you welcome.

In summary, those of you who have worked diligently through this book with me and my Sacred Seven, I invite you now to embrace me with your deserved gift of higher vibration and then to embrace all eight of us, especially your own Primary Guardian Angel. Together we can create a synergy of Love and Light and truly you have become a partner to the angels. Who knows, you may even traverse the Amethyst Star Gate* with us to learn how to create a Light Body (Merkaba), if indeed you are incarnate at this time to take this mighty step, as part of your soul's purpose in this vital moment on your Mother Earth.

*See Love & Light Angel Cards

Chapter Twelve

How to go further on the Way of Love & Light

Building your angelic connections

You need do no more than ask the angels for the subliminal connections to them (Attunements) set up in this book, and I have suggested in the chapters how and when you can do this. However, if you like you can try connecting to Templa Mar with the angels, (see the Appendix). You can also read about Templa Mar and view the artwork, plus much more, in various published books and card sets of mine mentioned here. Also I give many other types and vibrational levels of healing Angelic Light Attunements in my e-Courses, including different Violet Fire Attunements.

Studying Angela McGerr Angelology

I teach different levels of angel courses, mostly on-line. These start simply, as with Melchisadec and his Sacred Seven, continue with the Rulers of the Elements and Colours, and then progress towards Ascension: how to create different types of Angelic Light Body which are extensions of higher self and enable powerful healing to be sent to Mother Earth and mankind for Ascension and beyond; these are my 21st Century e-Mystery Courses retrieving that ancient wisdom for All.

With each deeper step you can build your knowledge to create and expand your own spiritual and etheric Light Body horizontally and vertically into various Sacred Geometry shapes called Merkabas. All becomes possible through awakening the Crystalline Heart. Through your own, direct, Angelic Light energy connection that bridges Above and Below, through heart, you will be able to aid a host of angels to manifest pure sacred geometry energy of Spirit *continuously,* through root, heart and crown, and to send it out to benefit Mother Earth and All Life that is sentient.

Light Work of unlimited potential

You could voluntarily engage in Light Work with the angels; this means aiding them by manifesting high vibration energies of all Colours of Creation for healing (wearing The Coat of Many Colours). This involves healing of mankind, Nature Kingdoms, inner Earth Kingdoms, not forgetting the fabric of Earth herself and her elements that give us life, even helping to re-balance Divine Masculine and Feminine – spiritual abundance indeed. The point is to give is to receive, and the more you send out healing to others, the more you will receive yourself (the three-fold return); the further you go along the Way, the further there is to go.

So far I have found unlimited potential to the Light Work we can choose to engage in with angels, as they can manifest as Angelic Light vibrations on Earth for those who can access these, but they need our assistance to ground the energy for All and bring it back through heart. Yet, as mentioned before, it is about our choices, decisions and actions. I hope this book will help inform *your* future choices in this respect!

You can refer to my website (see below) to see artworks of Melchisadec and his Sacred Seven, and a host of other angels, or follow the link from Home Page to my Blog, see more below. There is also a link there to the e-Course Programme to find out how to study my e-Modules or e-Mystery Courses; all take you further along the angels' Way of Love & Light.

Visit my website: angelamcgerr.com to see the angel artwork and learn more about healing self and life with angels (Heart & Soul Quests).

To see my nine previously published works (Quadrille Publishing) http://www.angelamcgerr.com/angelasexpertise.htm

Visit http://angelamcgerr.blogspot.co.uk/ to read my Blog, and click on More About Me to read, in two parts, how I was hijacked by angels in 1999 and what came after. Another link there takes you to information on my current e-Course Programme including the Angelic Light Body e-Courses: Ascension with Angels and Awakening the Crystalline Heart, and Blue Star and Emerald Table e-Mystery Schools

Follow me on Facebook: angelamcgerrauthor for timely angelic guidance messages, free healing visualisations, competitions, and my personal message facility. Also see that medium for notice of any UK or overseas events I am attending. I look forward to hearing from you.

Conclusion

To conclude, where exactly are you now, in terms of spiritual direction, as you read these words? It has been a privilege to assist you in making friends of Melchisadec and his Sacred Seven and in enabling you to invite them into your daily life. If you did so, you will have progressed considerably along the Way of Love & Light, and I hope you have attained a new level of physical and spiritual harmony. As Melchisadec says, you have reached another new beginning, and as the mystical Phoenix would point out, if you worked with the angels and did all the exercises, plus downloaded the Angelic Light Attunements, you are certainly at a higher vibration than you were before in the wonderful Dance of Six and Five. Also, you can do this all over again and as many times as you like.

Remember, the Dance continues to higher and higher levels of vibration, and with many more wonderful angels, as I explained in the General Introduction. As Melchisadec and I have said the choices are now and always were yours, although you can only make informed decisions from a position of increasing knowledge, experience and wisdom. Now that the Angels have illuminated the Way for you – will you go further?

Whatever you decide the Angels ask you to remember: Love is the Key

And Love gives healing form to Light through Sacred Geometry, for example:

Angel blessings always from
Angela McGerr

Appendix

About Templa Mar, The Beloved Temple of the Emerald Sea, and more on the Angelic Light Attunements

The Attunements are given, or you could say, channelled, through a crown, heart and root interface to Templa Mar, although in reality I am only *facilitating the angels who give them*. Templa Mar is the etheric Temple of Healing (The Beloved Temple of the Emerald Sea). It exists multi-dimensionally in non-linear Time, and has many names. We can go to Templa Mar each day to do our own meditations once we know how, and if we will and intend to do so, the angels will always help us. You will have seen the Templa Mar artwork if you have my *Heart & Soul Cards, Angel Quest of the Heart, or Love & Light Angel Cards* and you will in that case have already read the text about it – or you may have drawn one of the relevant cards that feature this sublime Temple. You can also view this on my website www.angelamcgerr.com

Now we are post 2012, here is an updated explanation about Templa Mar:

Temple of the Emerald Sea (*Updated from Heart & Soul card text*)

The Temple of the Emerald Sea is also Templa Mer (or Mar), the Beloved Temple, which has existed for All Time. Guarded by Metatron and Shekinah and interfacing with their Sacred Eden Tree, it is an etheric place of ultimate spiritual enlightenment, redressing the spiritual balance and vibration of Oneness lost from our world through the Falls, but which is now (post 2012 and by the grace of a critical mass of mankind towards Ascension) in process of being restored. The Ascension Programme applies not only to mankind, but also to Mother Earth and her Nature/Animal/Devic and Faerie Kingdoms, for the raising of the vibrational levels to restore planetary harmony to its original, pure, vibration involves choosing to heal by all souls and sentient beings: animal, vegetable and mineral, plus the Elements of Earth and her fabric itself.

Templa Mar is outside Time and Space and is a place of healing in every aspect and at the highest levels; its hallowed ground holds the pure harmonic fractals of 5, 6, (Dance of Six and Five) 12 and 13 (Higher Dance) in pure Light Codes: colour and sound, therefore potentially linking us back, through our own individual healing codes to our original (Divine Gem-Self – Adam Kadmon DNA) the vibration before our fall from grace. For each one of us our personal healing codes are there, at Templa Mar, waiting for us to choose to retrieve them. Thus Templa Mar helps the angels and other Light Beings to hold this blueprint for us through Ascension and beyond.

Therefore, all ancient souls will be drawn here. Through loving will and intention you can learn how to find the Way through the Star Gate of the Heart, to link your own higher heart to work with the Temple's Redemption programme. Once there, the High Priest, Seraphim and other Angels, Mystical Animals, higher Elementals and Nature Devas will instruct you in some of the ancient wisdom of the Mystery Schools, if you wish to use this to benefit All. The Mystery Schools (linked to 777 and 77:77) have operated, often secretly, throughout time to ensure this wisdom was retained, to be taught or remembered by those like yourself, whose soul's purpose was, is and ever shall be to tread the crystalline geometry pathways of healing that emanate from the Diamond Seed of Life in the higher heart for All.

Axis Mundi Books provide the most revealing and coherent explorations and investigations of the world of hidden or forbidden knowledge. Take a fascinating journey into the realm of Esoteric Mysteries, Magic, Mysticism, Angels, Cosmology, Alchemy, Gnosticism, Theosophy, Kabbalah, Secret Societies and Religions, Symbolism, Quantum Theory, Apocalyptic Mythology, Holy Grail and Alternative Views of Mainstream Religion.